LITERATURE
IN THE MODERN
WORLD

BLOCK 6
NEW WRITINGS
IN ENGLISH

*Prepared for the course team
by Dinah Birch, Angus Calder,
Graham Martin
and Dennis Walder*

GW00471707

A 3 1 9

Arts: a third
level course

The Open
University

The course team

Richard Allen (author)
Jenny Bardwell (BBC)
Richard Bessel (author)
Dinah Birch (author)
Angus Calder (author)
Kate Clements (editor)
Tony Coe (BBC series producer, author)
Charles Cooper (BBC)
Tony Coulson (Library)
Abigail Croydon (editor)
Roger Day (author)
Andrew Ferguson (course manager)
Margaret Harvey (block rapporteur)
Cicely Palser Havely (author)
Pam Higgins (graphic designer)
G.D. Jayalakshmi (BBC)
Denis Johnson (tuition group chair)
Maggie Lawson (Project Control)
Beth Martin (BBC)
Graham Martin (course team chair, author)

Mags Noble (BBC)
W.R. Owens (editor of anthologies)
John Pettit (editor)
Michael Rossington (author)
Sue Staig (secretary)
Betty Talks (BBC)
Nora Tomlinson (tuition group)
Dennis Walder (author)
Keith Whitlock (author)
Amanda Willett (BBC)
Richard Wilson (block rapporteur)

Consultants

Dr Pamela Morris, member of the Open University's teaching and counselling staff (block assessor)
Professor Michael Wood, department of English literature at the University of Exeter (external assessor)

The Open University

Walton Hall, Milton Keynes MK7 6AA

First published 1991

Typeset in 10 on 12 point Palatino

Printed in the UK by Courier International Ltd, Tiptree, Essex

ISBN 0 7492 1040 0

This block is part of an Open University course. The complete list of blocks is given at the end of this binding.

If you have not enrolled on the course and would like to buy this or other Open University material, please write to Open University Educational Enterprises Ltd, 12 Cofferidge Close, Stony Stratford, Milton Keynes MK11 1BY, United Kingdom.

If you wish to enquire about enrolling as an Open University student, please write to The Admissions Office, The Open University, PO Box 48, Walton Hall, Milton Keynes MK7 6AB, United Kingdom.

1.1

2400C/A319b6i1.1

Contents

Required reading

Chinua Achebe (1962) *Things Fall Apart*, Heinemann, first published 1958 (set book)

Wole Soyinka (1971) *Madmen and Specialists*, Methuen (set book)

Derek Walcott, *Another Life*, Chapters 7, 11 and 20, and 'The Schooner *Flight'* (in the Poetry Anthology)

Grace Nichols, poems (in the Poetry Anthology)

V.S. Naipaul (1973) *In a Free State*, Penguin, first published 1971 (set book)

R.K. Narayan (1982) *The Painter of Signs*, Penguin, first published 1976 (set book)

From the A319 Reader

Chinua Achebe, 'Colonialist criticism'

Chinweizu, Onwuchekwa Jemie and Ihechukwu Madubuike, 'Decolonizing African literature'

Elaine Savory Fido, 'Macho attitudes and Derek Walcott'

Edward Said, 'Yeats and decolonization'

(The A319 Reader is *Literature in the Modern World*, edited by Dennis Walder, 1990, Oxford University Press/The Open University.)

Broadcasts/cassettes

TV10 *'Madmen and Specialists' by Wole Soyinka* (linked to Section 3)

TV11 *Caribbean Poetry: the oral and literary traditions* (Section 4)

TV12 *Born into Two Cultures: Chinua Achebe and R.K. Narayan* (Sections 2 and 6)

TV14 *Changing Voices* (Section 4)

Radio 11 *Histories and Traditions: Wole Soyinka's 'Madmen and Specialists'* (Section 3)

Radio 12 *'In a Free State': a discussion* (Section 5)

Audio-cassette 3 Side 2, 'Walcott's "The Schooner *Flight*"' (Section 4)

(See also the Broadcast and Cassette Notes.)

Aims and objectives

This block has three principal aims:

(a) to show by the study of a selection of major texts from abroad the phenomenal upsurge in literary creativity in English in countries formerly part of the British Empire;

(b) to show by a discussion of certain key themes (history, identity, exile, language and the sense of place) the contribution of these 'new writings in English' to a redefinition of the English literary canon;

(c) to show by the inclusion of a range of literary forms, voices and countries the richness and variety of these 'new writings'.

1 Introduction

Redefining the canon

1.1 Much of the best writing in English today comes from outside the United Kingdom. Indeed the importance of North American literature, for example, has long been recognized, but this is not the case for literature from Africa, the Caribbean or Asia. And yet, since the Second World War and their growth towards independence, countries formerly part of the British Empire have produced an upsurge in literary creativity that should be hard, if not impossible, for any student of English literature – not to mention ordinary readers – to ignore. In this block we are going to present and discuss some of this 'new' writing, and to suggest why it is important in terms of its themes and techniques, and as a contribution to redefining the literary 'canon'.

1.2 By the time you have worked through the texts and our discussion, you should have a better idea of the nature and quality of the 'new writings in English', and have begun to develop an approach to them. Inevitably, we have had to be very selective; none the less, you should find yourself questioning traditional assumptions about the canon of English literature since, by its very origins, this 'new' body of work doesn't fit into that canon. It is as a challenge to literary and cultural hegemony that the novels, poetry and drama written and produced 'abroad' are taken up in this block.

1.3 There have already been several attempts to challenge that canon, but you may come to question their basis. For example, one influential textbook, *Society and Literature 1945–1970* (Sinfield, 1983), claims to challenge the 'enforced orthodoxy' (p.8) of literary studies by drawing on the new modes of understanding literature and culture that have come into play in recent decades – and that we are trying out with you on A319. Yet no single text in English from abroad is mentioned in Sinfield's book. The same absence is apparent in any number of recent critical attempts to oppose or subvert prevailing orthodoxies, from Catherine Belsey's *Critical Practice* (1980) to Terry Eagleton's *Literary Theory* (1983). Volume 8 of the *New Pelican Guide to English Literature* (Ford, 1983) seems an exception – containing, as it does, chapters on 'V.S. Naipaul and the politics of fiction', 'Two Nigerian writers: Chinua Achebe and Wole Soyinka' and 'India and the novel'. But the writers and works discussed in these chapters are barely mentioned elsewhere in the volume, and *not at all* in the introductory overviews of 'The social and cultural setting' and 'The literary scene', where you would expect at least some recognition of their presence and its implications for English studies. It's as if they are, instead, consigned to ghettos. The inclusion of, for example, Edward Said's account of 'Yeats and decolonization' in Part One of our Reader suggests at least one alternative approach.

1.4 Now it is a major aim of A319 to show how literature, mainly but not exclusively in English, has registered the larger changes of the modern world. One of those changes has been the decline of Britain as a world power – a decline marked by an increasing preoccupation with domestic affairs, and a disillusion with the country's former imperial role. It is often argued that, while losing political and economic leadership, Britain has maintained a certain cultural predominance through such institutions as the Commonwealth, and by the development of English as a world language.

1.5 But, since the early sixties, British influence within the Commonwealth has also declined, while the spread of English since the Second World War has had to do with US power rather than British. These facts are familiar, but they do help explain the persistence of a rather defensive, inward-looking ideology of Englishness – an ideology apparent not only in the narrowly domestic perspective of most recent UK writing but also in the extent to which apparently subversive, anti-traditional critics still silently assume that the only texts worth discussing are those produced solely within this country.

1.6   This, as I've suggested, is to ignore the quite remarkable growth in the literature produced by countries until relatively recently under the sway of the British – in Africa, Asia and the Caribbean. (A glance at French or Spanish literature today would show that this development is typical of writing not only in English.) Moreover, there are long traditions in *indigenous* languages that go back centuries before the rise of the ex-colonial nation-states whose borders now confine their many cultures; but it is writing *in English* that concerns us here. If we consider the literatures produced in those parts of the Empire that have long been settled by the British, such as Canada, Australia or South Africa, this would also reveal a substantial and interesting body of writing in English; but it is *new* writing in English that concerns us here. These 'new writings' are new not only in that the nation-states from which they have come are new, but also in the sense that they show the new styles and themes, the new creative *energies* that have accompanied the emergence of the countries of their origins from imperial rule.

What's new about 'new writings'?

1.7   You'll have seen that A319 challenges certain accepted notions of English literature. Is *A Passage to India* an 'English' novel? If so, in what sense? Not in setting, certainly. And in theme? It is at least arguable that the novel involves a profound response to the experienced 'otherness' of India – a place and a civilization that in history, complexity and sophistication implicitly challenged the authority of those who took it upon themselves to run it. In the end, Forster's novel sidesteps the conflict, attempting instead to redefine English liberalism for an English audience; and it is unable to escape its English perspective, in which the foreign becomes an arena for the exploration of native English concerns. But at least, unlike the preceding English literary texts we have looked at, *A Passage to India* registers the human existence of Indian people and their country, and goes beyond merely responding to difference as the exotic.

1.8   This is still a long way from the perspective of the writers whose work we will be looking at here. The basis of their view may be found in an autobiographical comment by the Nigerian novelist, Chinua Achebe, whose first work, *Things Fall Apart* (1958), we will be looking at in Section 2. There is a key, repeated phrase in the following account of how the writer came to write. Can you identify it?

> The Nationalist movement in British West Africa after the Second World War brought about a mental revolution which began to reconcile us to ourselves. It suddenly seemed that we too might have a story to tell. 'Rule Britannia!' to which we had marched so unselfconsciously on Empire Day now stuck in our throat.
>
> At the university I read some appalling novels about Africa (including Joyce Cary's much praised *Mister Johnson*) and decided that the story we had to tell could not be told for us by anyone else no matter how gifted or well intentioned.
>
> (Achebe, 1988, p.25)

1.9   Why did he find *Mister Johnson* appalling? First published in 1939, it depicted with wonderful comic zest the life of a semi-educated clerk who helped his white district officer to build a road in remote Northern Nigeria in the name of progress, only to end up shot like a sick dog. It was an advance upon the belittling stereotype of black people in earlier fictions of empire, such as Rider Haggard's *King Solomon's Mines* (1885), John Buchan's *Prester John* (1910), Edgar Wallace's *Sanders of the River* (1911) and even (although this is more debatable) Joseph Conrad's *Heart of Darkness* (1899). But the novel inevitably became offensive, its central character a stage black speaking bad pidgin. More important, as Achebe points out, it could not tell, in the repeated phrase, the story they had to tell.

History and new writings

1.10   Until the withdrawal of British rule, the colonized appeared to accept that they were always the objects of someone else's story. For 'story' we can understand 'history', too. The *retrieval of history* is the first and one of the most important issues in this block; it is also a central thread in the blocks that follow. Many women writers have argued that they, too, are involved in a process of rewriting history, as you will see in the next block. And the sense in which texts may be said to reinterpret or at least engage with 'history' as only one of many actual or potential discourses, is obviously crucial for understanding, say, Brecht's *Mother Courage.*

1.11   But for writers like Achebe, 'history' is more than a process requiring retrieval or reinterpretation: it is also *the source of an identity*. This is why, for example, autobiography has been from early on a favoured genre among the new African writers – return to a remembered childhood being one of the most telling means of summing up the past, including the 'traditional', pre-colonial tribal past, in order to find some shape for a life within the confusions and uncertainties of the present. This is an obvious element in Achebe's *Things Fall Apart*, of which the writer has remarked that 'although I did not set about it consciously in that solemn way', the novel was 'an act of atonement with my past, a ritual return and homage of a prodigal son' (1988, p.25). The novel recounts events that took place at the time of his grandfather, who was Igbo (Achebe's preferred recent usage, rather than 'Ibo'). This man's son (Achebe's father) was converted to Christianity by the missionaries and became a schoolteacher and evangelist, while many relatives and neighbours remained attached to Igbo religion and customs. Wole Soyinka's early upbringing, as detailed in *Aké: the years of childhood* (1981), involved a similar, complex mix of English-Christian and indigenous beliefs and cultures, although he came from a different Nigerian tribal group, the Yoruba.

1.12   If they cannot draw on their people's inheritance in any easy or uncomplicated way, at least these Nigerian writers have *had* an indigenous culture to draw on. For the Caribbean writer, the situation has been quite different. As the Trinidadian historian, the late C.L.R. James, pointed out:

> The West Indies has never been a traditional colonial territory with clearly distinguished economic and political relations between two different cultures. Native culture there was none. The Aboriginal Amerindian civilization had been destroyed. Every succeeding year, therefore, saw the labouring population, slave or free, incorporating into itself more and more of the language, customs, aims and outlook of its masters.
>
> (James, 1963, p.405)

1.13   Hence, for writers from the Caribbean, a more radical view has arisen out of their experience of colonialism – which involved the virtual extinction of the local population, and its replacement by slaves and indentured labourers from Africa and Asia. For such writers, as Derek Walcott says, 'history is fiction, subject to a fitful muse, memory'; and if they can 'contemplate only the shipwreck' of their world, they also experience 'an oceanic nostalgia for the older culture and a melancholy at the new' (Walcott, in Baugh, 1978a, pp.38, 42). Walcott himself comes from a tiny island whose control swung fourteen times between the French and the British before becoming the independent Commonwealth state of St Lucia. Perhaps it is not surprising that he should seek to forge a new present and future out of many pasts, rather than attempting the futile task of retrieving his own.

1.14 Walcott's position may be better understood in the terms adopted by the Martiniquan Frantz Fanon (1925–61) before him. Fanon is best known for his influential study of the Algerian revolution and its implications for Third World intellectuals, *Les Damnés de la terre* (1967, *The Wretched of the Earth*). In it, he argued that Third World writers went through three stages in their relations with the dominant, colonial culture: assimilation, reinterpretation and, finally, a 'revolutionary', 'national' phase (see 'On national culture', Reader, pp.270–71). What he means by this last phase is not entirely clear. Fanon believed that the Marxist interpretation of history had to be 'stretched' when applied to the colonial experience; in particular, the problem of racism had to be taken into account. So, while admitting that the 'Negro, however sincere, is a slave of the past', he also went on to argue that 'None the less I am a man, and in this sense the Peloponnesian War is as much mine as the invention of the compass … what I have to recapture is the whole past of the world'. For Fanon it is insufficient to 'dedicate myself to the revival of an unjustly unrecognized negro civilization' (1986, pp.225–6). Walcott's astounding range, through which he redefines himself simultaneously as a Caribbean artist and a figure in world history, suggests how far Fanon's words still ring true. But for V.S. Naipaul, the history, the cultures of 'New' and 'Old' Worlds alike, are insufficient: they offer no escape, much less a fruitful redefinition of humankind's place in the world. For him, it is the condition of *exile* – another key issue in this block – that defines the individual; the rest seems illusory. To this extent Naipaul situates himself within a familiar Modernist tradition – the tradition of writers such as Pound and Joyce, whose formal inventiveness and experimentation, whose concentration on the power of language, seem to have sprung from a parallel experience of dislocation and cultural rootlessness.

A common predicament?

1.15 And yet, when we consider the 'new writings' generated by such differences of position and experience, of historical and cultural inheritance, it soon becomes clear how far these differences have been fruitful rather than limiting, productive rather than paralysing. This may be because, as the Barbadian George Lamming summed it up in his significantly titled autobiography, *The Pleasures of Exile* (1960),

> What the West Indian shares with the African is a common political predicament: a predicament which we call colonial; but the word colonial has a deeper meaning for the West Indian than it has for the African. The African, in spite of his modernity, has never been wholly severed from the cradle of a continuous culture.
>
> (Lamming, 1960, p.34)

1.16 Whether individual West Indians or Africans would agree or not, the point is that this registers a cultural position, a set of feelings about themselves, that characterizes the 'new writers' in English. Derek Walcott and V.S. Naipaul offer different perspectives on the fundamental problem that confronts the 'colonial writer': how to overcome the negative effects of colonialism – including the cultural presumption and racism that survive its passing – while pursuing their art.

1.17   Thus, in his long autobiographical poem, *Another Life* (1973, part of which is in the Poetry Anthology), Walcott explores his own life, entering 'the house of literature as a houseboy' in order to find new beginnings, to rejoice in 'Adam's task of giving things their names'. But when Naipaul contemplates his own past, he finds only confusion and uncertainty, a confusion and uncertainty lodged in the very language he uses. As he confessed early in his career, in an article first published in 1965:

> To be an Indian from Trinidad is to be unlikely. It is, in addition to everything else, to be the embodiment of an old verbal ambiguity. For this word 'Indian' has been abused as no other word in the language; almost every time it is used it has to be qualified. There was a time in Europe when everything Oriental or everything a little unusual was judged to come from Turkey or India. So Indian ink is really Chinese ink and India paper first came from China. When in 1492 Columbus first landed on the island of Guanahani he thought he had got to Cathay. He ought therefore to have called the people Chinese. But East was East. He called them Indians, and Indians they remained, walking Indian file through the Indian corn ...
>
> (Naipaul, 1976, p.36)

1.18   Trapped by this sense of existential ambiguity, Naipaul went on to become one of the bitterest critics of his own world, 'a borrowed culture' as he calls it – the Mediterranean of the New World, but a Mediterranean 'where civilization turned satanic' and where the 'paternalism of colonial rule' seems likely to be replaced only by 'the jungle politics of rewards and revenge, the textbook conditions for chaos' (1962, pp.73, 224, 254).

1.19   Naipaul's corrosive criticism of post-independence societies sets him apart from other 'new writers' in English, and not only in the Caribbean. Of course, he is not alone in criticizing the culture, and especially the politics, of his place of origin. Achebe's view of contemporary Nigeria was summed up in a polemical pamphlet in which he asked his countrymen,

> Why is it that our corruption, gross inequities, our noisy vulgarity, our selfishness, our ineptitude seem so much stronger than the good influences at work in our society? Why do the good among us seem so helpless while the worst are full of vile energy?
>
> (Achebe, 1983, p.2)

1.20   The echo of Yeats in that last question is all the more telling from an author become one of his country's most famous sons for a novel taking its title from Yeats' great poem, 'Things Fall Apart'; and the criticism continues in Achebe's more recent work, including his 1988 novel, *Anthills of the Savannah*. Soyinka has, if anything, been even more ferocious in his attacks on Nigerian corruption and complacency; and indeed, the playwright was held in solitary confinement for nearly two years for attempting single-handedly to overthrow the regime that had plunged his country into civil war. He emerged with a damning indictment of the authorities in the form of a prison diary and the play, *Madmen and Specialists*, which he first produced in the USA at the start of five years' self-exile. These writers are far from accepting the post-independence status quo.

1.21   More alienating to Caribbean audiences, however, is Naipaul's lack of allegiance to the reconstruction of cultural values that engages most of the 'new writers'. *Commitment* is an even more important issue for them than it was for European writers between the First and Second World Wars. For all his later disillusion with his society, Achebe's motivation has remained grounded in this spirit:

> here then is an adequate revolution for me to espouse – to help my society regain belief in itself and put away the complexes of the years of

denigration and self-abasement ... The writer cannot expect to be excused
from the task of re-education and regeneration that must be done.

(Achebe, 1988, p.30)

Again, this is because, unlike the Caribbean writer, most African writers still
feel they have a culture, or set of traditions, they wish to call on, however
disturbed those traditions have been by foreign rule and the imposition of
foreign culture, as well as the successive traumas of post-colonial
development.

1.22   The sense of a continuing cultural tradition is more evident in the
writings of R.K. Narayan than in perhaps any African text we might have
chosen. Narayan's own view is that India will always remain a cultural unity
through its 'sacred books', some of which, for example the great epic
Ramayana, he has translated into English. These books, he says, are

> read ... all through one's life with a fresh understanding at each stage. Our
> minds are trained to accept without surprise characters of godly or demonic
> proportions ... With the impact of modern literature we began to look at
> our gods, demons, sages and kings, not as some remote concoctions but as
> types and symbols, possessing psychological validity even when seen
> against the contemporary background.
>
> (quoted in Rao, 1971)

1.23   Narayan's apparently unflurried acceptance of the continuity of one
culture in the face of another has led Naipaul to remark sarcastically that he
'tells an Indian truth. Too much that is overwhelming has been left out; too
much has been taken for granted' (1968, p.216).

1.24   Coming from a transplanted Indian background himself, Naipaul may
be expected to find a certain complacency in Narayan's rooted Indian view.
But the point is also that the Indian experience is so very different from his
own. The great Sanskrit epics referred to by Narayan are earlier than Homer,
a fact that helps remind us of the exceptional continuity and survival of the
cultures of the subcontinent, compared with those in the Caribbean or, to
some extent, Africa – although Africa has its great surviving epics too, such as
the story of *Sundiata*, founder of the Manding Empire of Mali during what is
known to Europeans as the Middle Ages (see the Reader, 'Decolonizing
African literature', p.283). It is sometimes suggested that the 'new writings in
English' were established earlier in India than elsewhere in the Empire, but
this is debatable, and depends on what is meant by 'new', since literary works
in English by Africans, for instance, were published as long ago as the
eighteenth century. What is agreed is that, just as the world-wide, anti-
imperial nationalist movements could claim their first real success with the
departure of the British from India in 1947, India was the first of the 'new' or
newly-independent nations to have a large and really established literature in
English – mainly novelists who had begun in the twenties and thirties,
including Narayan himself.

1.25   Despite such differences, for societies that have gone through the
profoundly disturbing shift from colonization to decolonization, an urgent
sense of commitment to common tasks is likely, perhaps inevitable, generating
shared areas of concern or themes. Such themes are shaped by their
originating places, by their very geography, as we see in the distinct emphasis
of many of the writings on the uniqueness of their environments, their so-
called *sense of place*. Thus, Narayan's novels may touch on issues common to
the new writings, such as the construction of an identity in situations of
cultural clash; but since the publication of his first novel as long ago as 1935,
he has stuck to the setting of an imaginary South Indian Tamil community
called Malgudi. In Malgudi, everything seems to be going on as it has for
centuries; and the calm texture of everyday life in the community is both

vivid and believable. Ironically, in the novel we have chosen to study here, *The Painter of Signs* (1976), there are indications that even Malgudi has changed, at last. The further irony, however, is that this supremely solid 'Indian' locale is created through the medium of a novel written in English.

New writings in *English*?

1.26   Indeed, the profound irony for *all* these writers is that they choose to tell their story, their history, in the *language* and, to a greater or lesser extent, by means of the cultural forms introduced by the colonizer whose dominating presence had negated their own. This is more obviously a continuing problem for African writers, readers and critics than for their Asian or Caribbean counterparts, for different reasons.

1.27   The Nigerian critics Chinweizu, Jemie and Madubuike point out that until there is a change in the circumstances that made Western languages the official African languages, 'it is pointless debating whether or not to use these Western languages in our literature' (1980/5, p.242); while the Kenyan Ngugi wa Thiong'o asks, 'What is the difference between a politician who says Africa cannot do without imperialism and the writer who says Africa cannot do without European languages?' (1986, p.26). Chinweizu carries on writing in English; Ngugi has written in his own Gikuyu since 1977, as well as in English. The fact that Nigerian independence (1960) emerged gradually and peaceably from under the system of 'indirect rule', while in Kenya self-rule (1963) came rapidly and as a result of bloody conflict with white settlers, may have a lot to do with these differences of attitude. So, too, may the fact that cultural contact between West Africa and Europe was more firmly and continuously established than in East Africa, as the long tradition of West African prose writing in English (over two centuries) reveals.

1.28   But the relationships between history, culture and language aren't so easy to disentangle. As Ken Ramchand points out, where English is a second language, the literature produced in that tongue is far from being the 'natural' expression of a whole society. And among the 'local factors' to be taken into account are the alternative literatures being produced in native languages, the number of people able to read English and what proportion of the total they represent, and the attitude of national governments to the foreign tongue (Ramchand, 1973, p.81). The Nigerian writer seeking a large audience, for example, needs to take into account that, in a country with a population of about 80 million, there are as many as 150 languages, none spoken by more than 6 or 7 million people – of whom the vast majority cannot read. In the West Indies, English is the *official* language of the five or six million people who inhabit the former British colonies, which may make the choice seem straightforward; but the language used by the mass of the people is Caribbean creole, and each country has its distinctive form.

1.29   We will be coming back to the question of language, which is clearly tied up with larger questions of history and culture as well as being central to the practical decisions that writers must take before they start writing. But it should at least be clear that the colonial experience, which inevitably involved the transplantation of Western European cultural forms, lies behind such questions; and indeed that, however different for different societies and communities, it has been a common factor for the writers we will be looking at here. And, above all, it has made their new writings available to us.

2 African voices I: 'Things Fall Apart'

A new voice?

ACTIVITY

Let's begin with beginnings. To get to grips with what Achebe was prompted to do (and why), we could look at the beginning of his novel and compare it with certain other beginnings. Read through the following extracts (the first of which should already be familiar), and give brief answers to these questions. Refer to the words of the passages as far as possible:

(a) What is the predominant *method of narration* in each passage?

(b) What is the *tone*, or attitude to its subject? (It may help if you read the passages aloud.)

(c) What *kind* of novel is this? Traditional-realist? Modernist?

(d) What would you say is *new* about the last passage?

> Except for the Marabar Caves – and they are twenty miles off – the city of Chandrapore presents nothing extraordinary. Edged rather than washed by the river Ganges, it trails for a couple of miles along the bank, scarcely distinguishable from the rubbish it deposits so freely. There are no bathing-steps on the river front, as the Ganges happens not to be holy here; indeed there is no river front, and bazaars shut out the wide and shifting panorama of the stream. The streets are mean, the temples ineffective, and though a few fine houses exist they are hidden away in gardens or down alleys whose filth deters all but the invited guest. Chandrapore was never large or beautiful, but two hundred years ago it lay on the road between Upper India, then imperial, and the sea, and the fine houses date from that period. The zest for decoration stopped in the eighteenth century, nor was it ever democratic. In the bazaars there is no painting and scarcely any carving. The very wood seems made of mud, the inhabitants of mud moving. So abased, so monotonous is everything that meets the eye, that when the Ganges comes down it might be expected to wash the excrescence back into the soil. Houses do fall, people are drowned and left rotting, but the general outline of the town persists, swelling here, shrinking there, like some low but indestructible form of life.
>
> (E.M. Forster, *A Passage to India*, 1924)

> The young women of Fada, in Nigeria, are well known for beauty. They have small, neat features and their backs are not too hollow.
>
> One day at the ferry over Fada river, a young clerk called Johnson came to take passage. The ferryman's daughter, Bamu, was a local beauty, with skin as pale and glistening as milk chocolate, high, firm breasts, round, strong arms. She could throw a twenty-foot pole with that perfect grace which was necessary to the act, if the pole was not to throw her. Johnson sat admiring her with a grin of pleasure and called out compliments, 'What a pretty girl you are'.
>
> Bamu said nothing. She saw Johnson was a stranger. Strangers are still rare in Fada bush and they are received with doubt. This is not surprising, because in Fada history all strangers have brought trouble; war, disease, or bad magic. Johnson is not only a stranger by accent, but by colour. He is as black as a stove, almost a pure Negro, with short nose and full, soft lips. He is young, perhaps seventeen, and seems half-grown. His neck, legs and arms are much too long and thin for his small body, as narrow as a skinned

rabbit's. He is loose-jointed like a boy, and sits with his knees up to his nose, grinning at Bamu over the stretched white cotton of his trousers. He smiles with the delighted expression of a child looking at a birthday table and says, 'Oh, you are too pretty – a beautiful girl'.

(Joyce Cary, *Mister Johnson*, 1939)

Okonkwo was well known throughout the nine villages and even beyond. His fame rested on solid personal achievements. As a young man of eighteen he had brought honour to his village by throwing Amalinze the Cat. Amalinze was the great wrestler who for seven years was unbeaten, from Umuofia to Mbaino. He was called the Cat because his back would never touch the earth. It was this man that Okonkwo threw in a fight which the old man agreed was one of the fiercest since the founder of their town engaged a spirit of the wild for seven days and seven nights.

The drums beat and the flutes sang and the spectators held their breath. Amalinze was a wily craftsman, but Okonkwo was as slippery as a fish in water. Every nerve and every muscle stood out on their arms, on their backs and their thighs, and one almost heard them stretching to breaking point. In the end Okonkwo threw the Cat.

That was many years ago, twenty years or more, and during this time Okonkwo's fame had grown like a bush-fire in the harmattan. He was tall and huge, and his bushy eyebrows and wide nose gave him a very severe look. He breathed heavily, and it was said that, when he slept, his wives and children in their out-houses could hear him breathe. When he walked, his heels hardly touched the ground and he seemed to walk on springs, as if he was going to pounce on somebody. And he did pounce on people quite often. He had a slight stammer and whenever he was angry and could not get his words out quickly enough, he would use his fists. He had no patience with unsuccessful men. He had had no patience with his father.

(Chinua Achebe, *Things Fall Apart*, 1958)

SAMPLE ANSWER

(a) The predominant method of narration is similar in all three passages and might be described in fairly conventional terms as omniscient, present-retrospective (although the present tense takes over in the second extract, and the past dominates in the third) and relatively 'distanced'.

(b) The tone of the first might be called 'civilized English observer' – descriptive, ironic, amused, judgemental: 'The streets are mean, the temples ineffective … whose filth deters all but the invited guest.' The tone of the second is equally knowing and detached, although more personal, perhaps. The observation that 'in Fada history all strangers have brought trouble; war, disease, or bad magic' suggests the amused, 'civilized' observer, who aims to amuse, too, by the characterization of the 'negro' Johnson. The tone of the last passage is the least judgemental, and is hardly humorous (although there is a hint of irony in the exaggerated account of Okonkwo's heavy breathing and springy step). The observer's relationship with the world described is more direct, serious and sympathetic.

(c) All three novels seem to conform to the traditional 'classic realist' model: we are expected to take each opening as an accurate account of the way things are, or were, in these particular settings. Indeed, there is a clear indication from the first words that we are being presented – at least initially – with ordinary, everyday reality: 'Chandrapore presents nothing extraordinary'; 'The young women of Fada, in Nigeria, are well known for beauty'; 'Okonkwo was well known…'

(d) This hardly seems a new *kind* of novel – and yet there is, perhaps, a new 'feel' to it? How is this conveyed? Are there any new *words* in it? Note down any that you haven't come across before.

DISCUSSION

What I am getting at here is the sense in which *Things Fall Apart* offers something 'new' to us. This seems to be less a matter of narrative method, or of the kind of fiction it offers, than of its tone, its feel. How do we begin to determine precisely the tone of a novel? By means of its *language*. The language of the opening of *A Passage to India* is that of a politely disdainful guidebook, isn't it? Balanced, neatly turned phrases ('The zest for decoration stopped in the eighteenth century, nor was it ever democratic') ironically note the arbitrary, alien customs of a foreign people ('as the Ganges happens not to be holy here'). The hint of mockery is developed in such a way as to invite the reader to collude with the 'civilized' point of view, the 'civilized' set of values, which finally judge the place and its people in that damning if faintly ambivalent last simile: 'like some low but indestructible form of life'. Of course, the hint of resistance to the 'civilized', knowing, English view implied by 'indestructible' becomes an important feature of the novel; but the English view remains the *dominant* voice.

The Cary passage, in concentrating more on the people than the place, may seem at first to be more sympathetic, offering their admittedly foreign value system at once: 'The young women of Fada, in Nigeria, are well known for beauty.' 'Well known', we are to take it, in Fada and the surrounding territory. And yet, by going on to describe the ferryman's daughter in terms of her 'skin as pale and glistening as milk chocolate' and her 'high, firm breasts', the narrator invites the (heterosexual male) European reader to share a certain system of values on terms that incorporate it within his own: the young woman is like a European delicacy and, we might note, not too black. Johnson, on the other hand, we are invited to think of as a pathetic clown, 'like a child', his body resembling 'a skinned rabbit's' and, significantly, 'as black as a stove'. Whereas an idealizing, exoticizing tone has crept in with the description of Bamu, Johnson is characterized in the more patronizing tone of the amused European encountering a half-educated black man. Either way, the Africans are rendered as less than human, their history a matter of 'war, disease, or bad magic'.

By contrast, the opening of *Things Fall Apart*, although 'detached' or 'objective' in tone, nowhere idealizes, exoticizes, belittles or undermines the values of the African culture it is describing. On the contrary, it is quietly but firmly positive about the world it is offering to the reader, apparently confident that we will understand – if not sympathize with – its values. Okonkwo's fame, we are informed, 'rested on solid personal achievements'. Yet the nature of those achievements – bringing 'honour' to his village by wrestling – is, of course, far from familiar or accepted in the culture out of which the authorial voices of E.M. Forster or Joyce Cary arise. And although in the third passage there is a distance between the authorial voice and its subject, this distance has to do with knowing more than any single character or group depicted, rather than with the cultural gulf evident in the earlier passages. In place of the arrogance and presumption of the knowing narrators of these passages, we have here an accepting intimacy that none the less does not – and this is very important in the light of what's to come – preclude criticism.

Perhaps 'tone' isn't quite the right word for this: it covers much more than immediately hits the eye, doesn't it? We've moved among cognitive, emotive and ideological elements in the mediation of the 'perspective' of each passage – the 'focalization', as Genette called it when clarifying the confusions surrounding the more traditional term 'point of view' (you might like to recall the discussion of these terms on Audio-cassette 1 Side 2). But it is hard, if not impossible, to avoid the entanglements of metaphor. The overriding consideration, what most makes the Achebe beginning seem 'new', is surely the perspective it adopts towards the culture it is presenting: the perspective of the narrator is *from within*. We are being introduced to the traditions of a community – its history, myths and culture – by a voice that, apparently, belongs to it. And it *sounds* like a *voice*, doesn't it, accommodating itself to being read aloud far better than the two other openings, the Forster and Cary 'voices'?

This is conveyed by a series of relatively short, syntactically simple and repetitively structured sentences, and by the comparisons that reflect an oral rather than a literate culture. Okonkwo's 'fame' has evidently been transmitted by word of mouth; Amalinze 'was called the Cat'; and 'the old man agreed' their wrestling-match was one of the fiercest 'since the founder of their town engaged a spirit of the wild for seven days and seven nights' – in other words, since the earliest times (whose history is transmitted as a myth or legend by the elderly men deputed to carry it on). As you may have noticed, the essential continuity of earthly and spiritual experience is implicitly accepted from the start; and so, too, are such 'pagan' customs as a man having several wives. This is also evidently a *male* perspective offered.

Did you notice that effective simile at the beginning of the third paragraph – 'Okonkwo's fame had grown like a bush-fire in the harmattan'? The point is, it's a comparison from *inside* the world being described, which helps to reinforce our sense of being in close contact with another culture, a culture that has its own frame of reference yet can be (and is) mediated to us by a narrator familiar with it. A colleague reading this for the first time thought 'harmattan' was a place; in the next paragraph but one, the narrator – characteristically – explains, as if merely in passing, that it is a cold and dry wind 'blowing down from the north'. It descends from the Sahara into the tropical zone of the continent each year during the dry season, drying out everything so that fires are frequent. According to Achebe, his wife

> who teaches English in a boys' school, asked a pupil why he wrote about winter when he meant the harmattan. He said the other boys would call him a bushman if he did such a thing ... I think it is part of my business to teach that boy that there is nothing disgraceful about the African weather, that the palm-tree is a fit subject for poetry.
>
> (Achebe, 1988, pp.29–30)

So the choice of 'harmattan' here is a deliberate step towards overturning the assumptions of cultural and racial inferiority imposed by the colonizers and accepted by the colonized, a step towards showing that the African words, their language, their whole way of life, have their own cultural integrity.

In short, to call this voice the voice of an omniscient narrator on the model of the traditional European novel does little justice to what we are being offered, and to its difference from what was formerly offered, especially in narrative fictions about empire. What is 'known' to the Forster and Cary voices – and what provides their basis for judgement – is English culture, which can also be understood to include a typically individualistic, literate, outsider's view of the Indian or African cultures being described. What is 'known' to the Achebe voice is *apparently* much more limited, although evidently new to English and, indeed, European culture. I say 'apparently' because, as we come to realize, the outside world *is* known to the narrator of *Things Fall Apart*, a novel that's a lot more subtle and complex than its 'simple' surface suggests. But more of that later.

2.1   In talking about the 'newness' of the voice we hear at the opening of *Things Fall Apart*, I have been assuming that its perspective is 'new' *to us*, its British audience. As we've seen, 'harmattan' is not a new word for Nigerians; and yet the text contains some explanation of its meaning after its first introduction. Does this suggest that the novel is written primarily for a nonlocal, overseas audience – indeed, for the same audience as *A Passage to India* and *Mister Johnson?*

2.2   The immediate answer seems to be yes. And this appears to be confirmed by the fact that *Things Fall Apart* was first published in Britain, by a British publisher, Heinemann, at a price few Nigerians could afford – fifteen shillings; and at a time (1958, two years before independence) when the local market for novels in English was severely limited – that is, even for novels whose status as set books in the English-run school system ensured some readership. Only a tiny minority of Nigeria's enormous multilingual and multicultural society was literate in English. But the answer is not quite so straightforward. Achebe's concern that Nigerian schoolchildren should not feel embarrassed into avoiding 'local' usages such as 'harmattan' suggests that he did – and does – have a local audience in view; and he has subsequently repeatedly insisted on the writer's responsibility to his own society, whatever the obvious and manifold difficulties. Further, the situation of the writer in English has by no means remained the same since the first appearance of *Things Fall Apart* in an expensive hardback abroad: shortly after independence in 1960, a cheap paperback edition appeared and then, in 1964, it became the first novel by an African writer to be included in the syllabus for African secondary schools throughout the English-speaking parts of the continent (except South Africa). The following year, Achebe himself reported proudly that the pattern of sales of the paperback edition (priced at five shillings) in the previous year had been as follows: 'about 800 copies in Britain; 20,000 in Nigeria; and about 2,000 in all other places' (1988 edn, p.28).

2.3   It is hard to overestimate Achebe's achievement. After immediate acclaim at home and abroad, *Things Fall Apart* remains the most important novel in the development of 'new' African writing in English. The book's status has long been assured, it has won its author numerous prizes and awards, it has been translated and read world-wide, and it has become a point of reference for all subsequent novels of Africa. This is not only a function of the way in which it registers the familiar experience of all the colonial or ex-colonial societies, although that is very important; but also, as we've seen, of its production – which in turn has been aided by its increasingly widespread acceptance, its status. There can be little doubt that its initial reception abroad, especially in the UK, was a crucial contributory factor, despite a somewhat condescending emphasis in the early reviews upon 'simplicity' and anthropological interest – an emphasis unfortunately encouraged by Achebe's next, and weaker novel, *No Longer at Ease*, which led a reviewer in the *New Statesman* to say that it was

> usual, almost traditional, to pay tribute to the simplicity of style of novels such as this. We tend to harp upon it, as if short words were something new in fiction. I suppose the fact of the matter is that simplicity is all we ask for in the African novel. We want a lucid, uncluttered account of the way life is changing in these territories … later, some very fortunate writers indeed will be able to fill the framework in, wallowing in the new luxuries of characterisation, motivation, depth psychology and all the rest of it.
>
> (Waterhouse, 1960, p.398)

2.4   'The fact of the matter is that simplicity is all we ask for in the African novel'! Really? Why? In the following week, historian Basil Davidson (reviewing Evelyn Waugh's *A Tourist in Africa*) remarked, 'At this stage of the argument, almost anything about African history is better than nothing'. And this, in an avowedly 'progressive', left-wing periodical that had long supported the African independence movements. This gives some sense of the dominant cultural presuppositions at the time in which Achebe's early writings appeared, a situation in which it could be taken for granted that almost anything about the African past was better than nothing.

2.5   But that situation has changed: there is now no excuse for condescending amazement at the appearance of such 'new' writings. The word 'new' here needs to be emphasized, since *Things Fall Apart* was by no means the first African novel in English, much less the first prose written by an African about Africa. The first *prose* by an African to be published in England may be found in the *Letters* (1787) of Ignatius Sancho, who began life aboard a slave-ship in mid-Atlantic and ended it as a corpulent Mayfair grocer and friend of Sterne, Garrick and Samuel Johnson. Even more remarkable is the autobiographical *Interesting Narrative of the Life of Olaudah Equiano* (1789), like Achebe an Igbo from eastern Nigeria, who, after buying his freedom from slavery, travelled widely as a merchant seaman, gentleman's valet and, finally, surgeon's assistant on an expedition to the Arctic. The first *novel* by a black African was probably the South African Solomon T. Plaatje's *Mhudi*, which was written in about 1917 and then published by the local missionary Lovedale Press in 1930. 'Probably', because there may be other candidates we don't know about, and also it could be argued – depending on your definition of 'novel' – that the first was *Ethiopia Unbound* (1911), part-autobiography, part-prophecy and part-fiction by the Ghanaian lawyer-statesman, E. Casely-Hayford. The first *extended prose fiction* by a West African did not appear until very much later: the Nigerian Amos Tutuola's *The Palm-Wine Drinkard* (1952), a wildly allegorical tale that was quickly succeeded by Tutuola's countryman Cyprian Ekwensi's more realistic *People of the City* (1954).

2.6 Rummaging in the lumber-room of literary history might sometimes seem to have little point. But at the very least it reminds us that works such as *Things Fall Apart* do not spring fully-fledged out of nowhere and, moreover, that from quite early on we are faced with certain questions: what do we mean by 'novel' in this context, what expectations do we have? The realist novel came into existence at a particular period in Western European history and as such it was shaped by literary conventions and complex cultural assumptions belonging to that time – which, of course, were not the same as those of Africans, then or now. Yet it is clearly one result of colonization – when societies and cultures intermingle – that Western literary forms have been adopted, just as the languages of the colonizers have been adopted. How, precisely, such adoption comes about depends on the specific situation of particular writers; but it should be obvious that the kind of education offered to, or imposed on, subject peoples has an enormous amount to do with it.

2.7 'What do African intellectuals read?', Achebe asked in an article in *The Times Literary Supplement*, providing the answer – little fiction and less literature, outside the school syllabus. This meant, in the 1950s,

> a couple of novels like *Pride and Prejudice, Wuthering Heights, Far Away and Long Ago*; one Shakespeare play, most likely *Julius Caesar* or *Romeo and Juliet*, and that would be all. In their class there might be a boy or two who had a flair for literature. Such people would pick up on their own some Peter Cheyney or Agatha Christie, but more likely Marie Corelli and Bertha Clay.
>
> (Achebe, 1972)

2.8 Marie Corelli and Bertha Clay?! In other words, not much 'high' literary culture. The position was improving at the time of writing, Achebe continued, there being more books around and more libraries than formerly. 'And what is more, the young reader can read something from African literature. We never had that.' What, then, did he have?

> When I was a boy things were rather different. Books were rare indeed; I remember the very strong impression made on me by the rows and rows of books in my school library when I first got there in 1944. I was, of course, most fortunate in gaining admission to a government college, one of those rare schools which the colonial administration built and endowed lavishly, for obscure reasons of its own. Cricket was played zealously and, in one of them at least, Eton Fives. But their most valuable asset was books. It is no doubt significant that, besides myself, almost all of the first generation of

Nigerian writers had gone to one of the four or five government colleges;
T.M. Aluko, Cyprian Ekwensi, Gabriel Okara, Wole Soyinka, J.P. Clark,
Christopher Okigbo, V.C. Ike, Nkem Nwankwo, Elechi Amadi.

> By contrast, the vast majority of schools had inadequate libraries or none at
> all. I was not to know fully what advantage we had until I went years later
> to teach in one of the so-called private schools in my district and discovered
> that the school 'library' consisted of a dusty cupboard containing one copy
> of the holy bible, five pamphlets entitled *The Adventures of Tarzan*, and one
> copy of a popular novel [by Marie Corelli] called *The Sorrows of Satan*
>
> (Ibid.)

2.9　This was the situation during and immediately after the Second World
War, when a newly wealthy and nationalistically-minded Nigeria was moving
towards independence. In 1948 University College, Ibadan (an extension of
London University, later to become the University of Ibadan), opened, and
was immediately hugely influential in the development of Nigerian literature.
Achebe (born 1930) and Soyinka (born 1934) were among those who attended,
and it was there that Achebe read those 'appalling novels' about Africa that
first set him writing (short stories, published in the Ibadan *University Herald* in
1952). The appearance of student journals, the establishment of literary-
cultural clubs and magazines such as *Black Orpheus*, helped secure the key role
that the Ibadan circle was to play in creating a new national Nigerian
literature – and, indeed, what has been called 'the first true national literature
in sub-Saharan Africa' (Lindfors, 1975, p.8).

2.10　Given the education system in pre-independence Nigeria and the lack of
interest by the colonial authorities in *African* writing, Achebe clearly could not
have read Plaatje's *Mhudi*, much less Equiano's autobiography. Indeed, even
today these works are only gradually becoming known outside specialist
departments. Yet both of them anticipate some of the concerns of *Things Fall
Apart*, especially its emphasis on the depiction of a traditional society under
pressure to change. As we know (see paragraph 1.8), what immediately
prompted the writing of Achebe's first novel was, instead, his reading at
Ibadan of those earlier fictions about Africa by whites, and in particular Joyce
Cary's *Mister Johnson*. What was it about *Mister Johnson* that provoked
Achebe's writing? The answer should be clear from our analysis of the
passages above: Cary's perspective is inevitably that of the outsider, however
sympathetic (and it is rather less sympathetic than it seems at first, isn't it?);
Achebe's perspective is that of the insider, who doesn't need to be
sympathetic. What he does is to take over and occupy the form, the 'realist
English novel', offered or imposed by the best of the colonial education
system. By doing so, he announces a new voice for his own people, and to the
outside world.

Reading *Things Fall Apart*: Chapter 1

2.11　You could now read the whole novel at one go; but for the moment, I
won't assume you have. Instead, I shall work through the earlier pages in
some detail. This is to ensure that we can agree about how it appears to ask
to be read, before considering the rest in as much or as little detail as seems
fitting or possible in this limited space.

ACTIVITY

Now please read the first chapter of Part One of *Things Fall Apart* (including
the epigraph). If you have not read it before, read it twice. What, simply, is it
about? How does the narrator's attitude towards his subject affect how we
respond to it? Are there any clues to the theme(s) of the story?

DISCUSSION

First let's consider the epigraph, from Yeats's 'The Second Coming' (discussed in Block 1), which also contains the phrase used for the title of the novel. This suggests a modern theme, doesn't it – of a certain order and tradition being displaced by disorder? And not merely disorder, but a cataclysmic 'anarchy', as of a whole civilization breaking up. Moreover, if you recall the poem, the vision it proposes is of a succession of civilizations, each containing the seeds of its collapse. Does the first chapter then go on to show how this theme is to be taken up? Only very indirectly; and yet it is there, as we shall see.

What the chapter is about on the level of character is obvious enough, perhaps. We are told about Okonkwo's father, Unoka the flute-player, whose 'lazy and improvident' ways made his son feel ashamed and determined to prove himself. This Okonkwo has done, by becoming a champion wrestler, fighting bravely in two inter-tribal wars, and building himself up to become a wealthy farmer with three wives and two barns full of yams. By his own efforts, Okonkwo has made himself one of the most important men in the nine villages of Umuofia. His prowess, his achievements, are, however, undermined a little, are they not? Not only by the hints of exaggeration about his heavy tread and breath; but also by the sternness and impatience that, as we are shown here, contrast so strongly with the 'feminine' qualities of his father, a feckless but gentle and persuasive man who prefers music and dancing, and the social skills beloved of his people, to the hard work and willingness to fight which they respect among men – hence Unoka's ignominious death.

The main subject of the opening chapter is less the individual make-up of these people, although that is important, than the way in which their character merges with and is defined by the life of the community. One example of how this is managed occurs when the narrative pauses to focus on a moment from the past, before the beginning of the story (an external *analepsis*, to use the more precise terminology to which you were introduced in Block 2 Section 3). This is also the longest extended scene in the opening chapter. It describes how Unoka dealt with a friend to whom he owed money:

> One day a neighbour called Okoye came in to see him. He was reclining on a mud bed in his hut playing on the flute. He immediately rose and shook hands with Okoye, who then unrolled the goatskin which he carried under his arm, and sat down. Unoka went into an inner room and soon returned with a small wooden disc containing a kola nut, some alligator pepper and a lump of white chalk.
>
> 'I have kola,' he announced when he sat down, and passed the disc over to his guest.
>
> 'Thank you. He who brings kola brings life. But I think you ought to break it,' replied Okoye passing back the disc.
>
> 'No, it is for you, I think,' and they argued like this for a few moments before Unoka accepted the honour of breaking the kola. Okoye, meanwhile, took the lump of chalk, drew some lines on the floor, and then painted his big toe. As he broke the kola, Unoka prayed to their ancestors for life and health, and for protection against their enemies. When they had eaten they talked about many things ...
>
> 'Thank you for the kola. You may have heard of the title I intend to take shortly.'
>
> Having spoken plainly so far, Okoye said the next half a dozen sentences in proverbs. Among the Ibo the art of conversation is regarded very highly, and proverbs are the palm-oil with which words are eaten ...
>
> (pp.4–5)

Kola, the slightly narcotic, caffeine-rich fruit of a West African tree, is used in Igbo social rituals – especially, as here, in greeting a guest. But do you need to be told that? Hardly. Or, perhaps more puzzling, 'Okoye … took the lump of chalk, drew some lines on the floor, and then painted his big toe'. The chalk, a kind of white clay, is also used extensively in social ceremonies: the lines are the visitor's 'personal emblem'. Painting his toe indicates he has taken the *ozo* title, available only to men of honour and wealth, and signifying entry into the eternal community of the clan (if he had taken higher titles, he would further mark his face). Robert Wren explains:

> The kola and chalk symbolise respectively the close bond between host and guest and their mutual benevolence. Okoye has, in fact, come on an unpleasant errand: he wishes to collect a debt. The ceremony ensures that the difficult subject will not arise in an atmosphere of rancour or antagonism. Okoye may or may not get what he wants (he does not), but the ceremony has precluded a quarrel.
>
> (Wren, 1980, p.28)

But, again, do we need this explanation? The meticulous, minute account of greeting more than suffices to make the point. The rich texture of everyday clan life has been vividly brought out, and not merely to suggest local 'colour'. It is evident that how the individual fits in with (or fails to fit in with) this living, local world counts as much as, if not more than, the depiction of the ceremony itself. And this is also part of a larger project of revealing in detail and in depth the formal, *orderly* nature of this society, thereby making us feel what is at stake if it should, as the title and overall theme already hint, be threatened by any changes.

This could not be further from the dark pagan mysteries, the primitive chaos, of European myth and stereotype concerning Africa – powerfully expressed even in Conrad's *Heart of Darkness* (1899), which showed the horrors of European imperialism in Africa, yet which depicted what it's like to go up the Congo river in these terms:

> suddenly, as we struggled round a bend, there would be a glimpse of rush walls, of peaked grass-roofs, a burst of yells, a whirl of black limbs, a mass of hands clapping, of feet stamping, of bodies swaying, of eyes rolling, under the droop of heavy and motionless foliage. The steamer toiled along slowly on the edge of a black and incomprehensible frenzy… It was unearthly and the men were – No, they were not inhuman. Well, you know, that was the worst of it – this suspicion of their not being inhuman.
>
> (Conrad, 1971, p.36)

The *mere possibility* of kinship to these howling savages, remarkable as it was for the time to suggest as much, none the less reveals an image of Africa as '"the other world", the antithesis of Europe and therefore of civilization, a place where man's vaunted intelligence and refinement are finally mocked by triumphant bestiality' (Achebe, 1988, p.2).

What we are offered instead in *Things Fall Apart* is an image of different, but human, beings – engaged in the custom, the 'ceremony of innocence'. Yeats's lines are being used ironically: they derive from a European vision that assumes order at home and anarchy abroad, whereas what we are shown here is order abroad. And when the Europeans do arrive, with their much-vaunted 'civilization' … but this is to anticipate. At this stage, it is already clear that this text is engaged in *retrieving the past* not just to recall the nature and functioning of pre-colonial society, but also to assert its human value. As Achebe wrote,

> The fundamental theme must first be disposed of. This theme – put quite simply – is that African people did not hear of culture for the first time

from Europeans; that their societies were not mindless but frequently had a philosophy of great depth and value and beauty, that they had poetry and, above all, they had dignity.

(Achebe, 1973)

And yet this society is not wholly 'innocent', it is not ideal: the opening chapter makes you realize that, doesn't it? For there is a certain one-sidedness, a certain rigidity about the tribe's value-system, as it is presented to us. Thus it is a society that does not (perhaps cannot) value the positive qualities displayed by Unoka, his gentleness, affability and humour; instead it heaps praise upon his stern son, with results clearly anticipated in the concluding paragraph of the chapter. If it is most important to recognize how far we have been taken from the familiar stereotyping of Africa and African peoples as inhuman, it is equally important to realize that this is not done by simply presenting us with an alternative stereotype, of Africans as superhuman, somehow not prey to the usual ills that flesh is heir to.

One of the ways in which this complexity is managed is by means of the construction of the narrator, whose own position is not easy to determine. At times, that narrator is so carefully effaced from what we are given, so detached, as to seem almost anthropological: 'Among the Ibo the art of conversation is regarded very highly, and proverbs are the palm-oil with which words are eaten.' This is very neat, isn't it? Using a proverb to explain the proverbial nature of Igbo conversation, it sums up a position that is simultaneously involved with and at a distance from his material, the tense implying that this is true in the narrative present and not only in the distant past of the story. And towards the end of the chapter, we are informed that

> When Unoka died he had taken no title at all and he was heavily in debt. Any wonder then that his son Okonkwo was ashamed of him? Fortunately, among these people a man was judged according to his worth and not according to the worth of his father. Okonkwo was clearly cut out for great things ...
>
> (p.6)

What we have here is a careful modulation – from plain, descriptive, external 'fact', through indirect reportage (although Okonkwo's shame is posed as a question), to the community view of 'among these people' that, again, is offered by a knowing outsider. The final sentence, however, is only straightforward on a quick first reading, as we begin to realize retrospectively when the slowly looming tragic irony of Okonkwo's fate emerges.

It is the care with which this narrative voice is controlled that largely determines the reader's growing, complex awareness of the forces at work in the society depicted. The sense of order, ritual and harmony – the predominant note of the opening chapter – is subtly counterpointed by the hints of a potential for tension and disturbance in the relationship between Unoka and his surrounding society, including his overbearing but impressive son, Okonkwo. The development of the whole novel is implied at the start, although of course that's not something one can confirm until reaching the end.

2.12   Before we go on to the rest of the novel, I want to stress the absolute conviction with which the world of Umuofia is conveyed from the beginning, since this is what enables us to accept its depiction almost unthinkingly. This culture is almost certainly wholly new to us, and simultaneously is distanced from its Nigerian readers by time and the changes wrought by colonialism. This convincing picture is of course a product of the language of the text – in particular, of the way in which it incorporates and familiarizes the unfamiliar, including unfamiliar words. I've mentioned how the slight strangeness of 'harmattan' is handled; that is succeeded by the introduction of the actual vocabulary of the community whose way of life is being defined – as in *egwugwu*, and then, after a few more paragraphs, 'the *ekwe* and the *udu* and the *ogene*' all at once, terms explained in the glossary at the back, although it is questionable whether readers abroad really feel the need for that explanation, so clear is the context, so gradual the process of introducing them.

2.13   I have lingered on the opening and first chapter because it is important to grasp the novel's basic method and its subject: this is less the development of individual character or plot than the revelation of a way of life, a way of life depicted as if it were entirely static and self-contained but which, the ironic hints of the title and first chapter suggest, is subject to inevitable change – in short, to human history.

2.14   It is only by fully recognizing from the start the novel's complex ambitions and achievement that we can avoid the trap of what Achebe himself calls 'colonialist criticism'. Many readers and critics of *Things Fall Apart* fell into (and some still do) this trap. A brief glance at the first few pages of Achebe's essay 'Colonialist criticism' (reprinted in the Reader, pp.271–9) will show you what is meant. Achebe was accused of an idealizing nostalgia, of mythologizing a violent and bloody past that the missionaries and district officers had helped to end. But right from the start it should be clear that the novel is far from offering some timeless, mythical account of African life; instead, time and myth are revealed as dimensions of a specific, and by no means perfect, African society. The difference is crucial. Before you tackle the debate in detail, however, you will need to have read further in the novel. We will come back to these issues later.

Reading *Things Fall Apart*: **The death of Ikemefuna**

ACTIVITY

Let's now speed up. Please read to the end of Chapter 7 (p.43). What is your response to the events there detailed? Does what happens confirm the implications of the opening? How have the accounts of the clan's ceremonies and rituals (for example in Chapter 6) contributed to the meaning of Ikemefuna's death?

DISCUSSION

My own feeling was one of shock and dismay at the killing of the boy Ikemefuna, and perhaps also anger at Okonkwo for not heeding the advice even of the respected village elder Ezeudu: 'That boy calls you father. Do not bear a hand in his death' (p.40). The boy's execution has been anticipated – not only by the last words of Chapter 1 ('the doomed lad') but by such reminders (typical of oral narrative) as 'whose sad story is still told in Umuofia unto this day' (p.9). So, too, although more subtly, has Okonkwo's involvement been anticipated – for example, by the way in which his impatience and quick temper tend increasingly to work against him, despite his hard work and fierce loyalty for the institutions of his clan. When his youngest wife, Ojiugo, neglects her domestic duties, he beats her:

> In his anger he had forgotten that it was the Week of Peace. His first two wives ran out in great alarm pleading with him that it was the sacred week. But Okonkwo was not the man to stop beating somebody half-way through, not even for fear of a goddess.
>
> (p.21)

The result of this impiety is that the priest of the earth goddess he has offended calls on him, refusing the customary offer of kola nut, to tell him that the 'evil you have done can ruin the whole clan' (words evidently loaded with prophetic implication). He has to pay a fine in compensation, and is 'inwardly repentant'; but the isolation consequent upon his proud refusal to share such feelings leads to his being called 'the little bird *nza* who so far forgot himself after a heavy meal that he challenged his *chi*' or personal god (p.22).

Another way of putting this (every proverb in the novel deserves scrutiny) might be to say that there is something essentially contradictory and self-defeating about Okonkwo's behaviour – although that is to assume that this is a function of his character alone, which it isn't since, as we've seen, character and community are in this novel inseparable. During the Feast of the New Yam, his frustration at the enforced inactivity leads him to beat one of his wives for a minor misdemeanour, then 'madly' try to shoot her for murmuring 'something about guns that never shot' (p.28). The comic element doesn't obscure the destructive potential of his impetuosity, nor the feeling of foreboding as such incidents accumulate. Chapter 6 gives an account of the ritual wrestling which brings out powerfully the renewed, joyful identification of individual and community, the drummers' 'frantic rhythm' becoming the 'very heart-beat of the people' (pp.35–6). But as Okonkwo's presence reminds us, harking back to the first chapter, it was precisely such early 'masculine' achievements as a wrestler that led to his high position in the tribe and hence the guardianship of Ikemefuna, now leading to a tragic outcome.

The interweaving of festivals and other communal activities with the behaviour of individual members of the clan is crucial if we are to accept the clan's rules – or at least to accept them sufficiently to understand why Ikemefuna has to be sacrificed (although, as we come to realize, that has been set up to underline the inflexibility, and hence vulnerability, of the clan ethic). The killing of Ikemefuna is a turning-point because it dramatizes this tension for the first time. It also provides the first example of extended narrative focus on the interior world of a character, all the more notable for having been preceded by the festivities of Chapter 6 and, in Chapter 7 itself, the communal spectacle of the arrival of the locusts in unexpected abundance.

It is therefore no coincidence that, just as Okonkwo sits happily crunching the rare food with the two boys he has come to love (Ikemefuna and his elder son Nwoye), Ezeudu arrives with the Oracle's ruling on the adopted boy's fate. The fateful journey that follows is described in powerful, haunting detail – the 'elusive' sound of a peaceful *ozo* dance from a distant clan rising and falling with the wind as the little group trudges on in silence. The 'short trees and sparse undergrowth' around their village give way to 'giant trees and climbers which perhaps had stood from the beginning of things' (p.41). The unexpected deepening of tone is amplified as we enter the boy's innocent, unsuspecting consciousness – his initial uneasiness quelled by his awareness of his foster father behind him, happily anticipating return to his original home with a childhood song, given in untranslated Yoruba. (The chorus is given to the non-Yoruba reader on page 25, 'where the ant holds his court in splendour and the sands dance for ever'; the earlier lines contain a warning to the king, *Eze*, not to eat – or face the consequences.)

> One of the men behind him cleared his throat. Ikemefuna looked back, and the man growled at him to go on and not stand looking back. The way he said it sent cold fear down Ikemefuna's back. His hands trembled vaguely on the black pot he carried. Why had Okonkwo withdrawn to the rear? Ikemefuna felt his legs melting under him. And he was afraid to look back.
>
> As the man who had cleared his throat drew up and raised his matchet, Okonkwo looked away. He heard the blow. The pot fell and broke in the

sand. He heard Ikemefuna cry, 'My father, they have killed me!' as he ran towards him. Dazed with fear, Okonkwo drew his matchet and cut him down. He was afraid of being thought weak.

(p.43)

To my mind this is almost intolerably moving, comparable with the great tragic moments in Sophocles or Shakespeare. Not only is this because of its apparently plain but powerful form of utterance, but also because of the complex resonances it sets up, which mark the beginning of the end for Okonkwo, and for the culture to which he belongs.

Can you see how these resonances are immediately confirmed by what follows Ikemefuna's death? We've been prepared from the start for the boy's unfortunate end, but without being told when or how exactly it will take place; similarly, we've been led to the realization that Okonkwo, for all his heroic qualities, is fatally flawed, although we cannot precisely predict the outcome; and finally, the accumulating hints of contradiction within the tribal ethic are now about to emerge with renewed and explicit force. First there is Nwoye's reaction:

> As soon as his father walked in, that night, Nwoye knew that Ikemefuna had been killed, and something seemed to give way inside him, like the snapping of a tightened bow … He had had the same kind of feeling not long ago … They were returning home with baskets of yams … when they had heard the voice of an infant crying in the thick forest … Nwoye had heard that twins were put in earthenware pots and thrown away in the forest, but he had never yet come across them. A vague chill had descended on him …
>
> (p.43)

The killing of Ikemefuna is, for Nwoye, connected with the tribe's harsh treatment of twins. This is the second time (following quickly on the first) that we have a close focus on the inner life of a character. And, significantly, it offers a second insight into the potential harshness towards individual life of the tribal or communal ethic. And again, as we shall see, it has a prophetic or *proleptic* function within the narrative.

Then we might notice that the next chapter opens with an Okonkwo startlingly reduced in stature, grieving for Ikemefuna, unable to eat, and drinking until his eyes are like a dying rat's. Yet he remains incapable of repudiating the morality he executed so fiercely, or of perceiving the compromise permissible within it. When his friend Obierika expresses the clan's view of his excessive loyalty to its masculine ethos, his response is unequivocal, unyielding, and the implications for the future of his people are clear: 'someone had to do it', he says. 'If we were all afraid of blood, it would not be done. And what do you think the Oracle would do then?' Obierika replies:

> 'You know very well, Okonkwo, that I am not afraid of blood; and if anyone tells you that I am, he is telling a lie. And let me tell you one thing, my friend. If I were you I would have stayed at home. What you have done will not please the Earth. It is the kind of action for which the goddess wipes out whole families.'
>
> 'The Earth cannot punish me for obeying her messenger,' Okonkwo said. 'A child's fingers are not scalded by a piece of hot yam which its mother puts into its palm.'
>
> 'That is true,' Obierika agreed. 'But if the Oracle said that my son should be killed I would neither dispute it nor be the one to do it.'
>
> (pp.46–7)

So even within the clan culture the results of Okonkwo's action can be thought of as threatening 'whole families'. As we shall see, there is even more at stake: the tensions between Okonkwo and his community reflect larger tensions within the clan ethic and, ultimately, they provide the point of weakness before the gathering, external forces of history in the form of the arrival of the whites. The point is reinforced by the evident inadequacy of Okonkwo's proverb to explain how things should be interpreted.

ACTIVITY

As is typical of a novel in which so much works proleptically (a feature that is itself part of the growing, overall irony of tone), the whites' arrival is anticipated long before it is depicted. Can you see where? What do you make of the end of Chapter 8?

SAMPLE ANSWER/DISCUSSION

The chapter concludes with a nicely ironic little conversation that turns to the world at large, in which other tribes do things differently: 'I have even heard that in some tribes a man's children belong to his wife and her family', remarks Okonkwo, something so improbable and unnatural as to remind Obierika of the story of 'white men who, they say, are white like this piece of chalk' and 'have no toes'.

> 'And have you never seen them?' asked Machi.
>
> 'Have you?' asked Obierika.
>
> 'One of them passes here frequently,' said Machi. 'His name is Amadi.'
>
> Those who knew Amadi laughed. He was a leper, and the polite name for leprosy was 'the white skin'.
>
> (p.52)

Up to now, the ironic overtones of the narrative have largely operated to limit or undermine the depiction of Okonkwo as the 'hero' of Umuofia, and in favour of the clan perspective – recalled here in the sideswipe at the strangeness of those who have white skins and wear shoes. But rather more important now is that level of 'historical' or 'cultural' irony which is beginning to work against the clan: for it will be precisely the outcasts and lepers who turn towards what the missionaries have to offer.

ACTIVITY

These anticipatory, ironic effects of course require for their full appreciation that you read the whole novel. So, if you have not already done so, *go ahead now* and read it through, keeping in mind the points I have raised about the manner and matter of its proceeding, and noting for yourself where they might be confirmed, modified or confounded. As you will see, the next few chapters apparently reaffirm the stable and harmonious equilibrium of individual, family and community, before the abrupt climax of this first part of the novel swings us back to an awareness of the contradictions inherent in their way of life, and the likely tragic outcome.

Structure and evaluation

2.15 Let's now look at *Things Fall Apart* as a whole. Achebe's novel ends with the title of a book by a white man, *The Pacification of the Primitive Tribes of the Lower Niger*. Thus legend has become history; but, more than that, one culture and way of life has been absorbed and redefined by another. Another way of putting this is to say that one history has been displaced by another. The ironic overtones are obvious and forceful, and reverberate in our experience of the cultural clash through which the narrative has taken us. The entire tragedy of Okonkwo and his people is going to be transformed, by the European outsider's patronizing interest, into a 'reasonable paragraph' in the book – doubtless for the edification of later Europeans *and*, it's relevant to realize, Nigerians brought up and educated within the British colonial system. Hence the need to rewrite, or retrieve that earlier history, an ambition central to Achebe's project.

2.16   I have been stressing the crucial effect of the shifts in narrative focus, and I'm sure you can see what a brilliant last move it is to take the reader into the district commissioner's consciousness for the closing chapter. Here we have, dramatized from within, the easy stereotyping of the colonizer's mind, its small ambitions obscuring and so denying the human complexity that we have come to know and understand through the narrative. The word 'primitive' precisely focuses all that is misguided about the outsider's viewpoint, simultaneously reminding the reader that what we have been reading is (although in 'our' language, English) a new register of English – proverbial, 'oral', formal, recreating Igbo speech and thought.

2.17   The conclusion also reminds us of the kind of truth that a novel – rather than a political pamphlet, historical document or anthropological treatise – can offer; which in turn brings out the profoundly paradoxical nature of Achebe's enterprise – apparently reaffirming the value of a European literary genre, while questioning the cultural perspective inherent in it.

2.18   And yet, doesn't *Things Fall Apart* largely conform to the familiar conventions of the European realistic novel? And if not, how should we define its achievement – in terms of that tradition, or in terms of some other, African or Nigerian or Igbo tradition? How do we, as readers of the novel abroad, ultimately respond to and evaluate it? The relevance of these questions in any discussion of *Things Fall Apart* seems clear from the novelist's own response to what he called the 'colonialist criticism' of his first novel, as well as from the more general argument in Chinweizu's now well-known critique of European approaches towards the 'new' writings, *Toward the Decolonization of African Literature*. These two essays, which we shall be looking at shortly, also propose some answers.

2.19   But before we proceed to this more general debate, we should clarify at least one more aspect of the novel – its *structure*. We can't separate considerations of structure and evaluation, as can be shown in the following comment by my colleague, Graham Martin, whose first reading led him to conclude that the novel makes 'one point only':

> Here's how I read it. Up to Chapter 15 and the arrival of the Christian missionaries, Okonkwo's story seems no more than a narrative device for presenting the way of life of his and similar Igbo clans. Different chapters are almost, in themselves, documentary short stories, each recounting some aspect of the 'culture' – farming practices, courtship and marriage rites, settling quarrels between villages (the death of Ikemefuna), ancestor worship, judicial process (the *egwugwu* decision about Uzowulu's wife), and so forth.
>
> Then follows, in effect, a straightforward *exemplum* that the Christian missionary is followed, as day by night, by alien 'law', and that the old life can't survive the combined assault. Christianity attracts enough support from the disaffected and outcast clan members to undermine traditional morale. Okonkwo's resistance and suicide underline the defeat.
>
> The effect of the final chapters is certainly chilling, and well summed up in the district commissioner's memorandum that this will provide him with good material for his book. The point that the way of life presented to us is, in its own way, valuable and impressive, and that the dismissive term 'primitive' is a piece of stupid and grotesquely patronizing ignorance, is effectively made. But beyond that ...?

ACTIVITY

Graham Martin goes on to agree with Angus Wilson's conclusion in *The Observer*, to the effect that it is a 'very simple but excellent novel', which, he says, 'sounds patronizing but isn't in the context'. What do you think? Is this an adequate account of the novel and its effect?

SAMPLE ANSWER/DISCUSSION

To some extent I gave you my answer when we dealt with the opening and early chapters of *Things Fall Apart*, touching on: the novel's use of language; the manipulation of narrative perspective; the treatment of history and cultural perception or identity; and the prevailing sense of tragic irony – all to suggest the integration of the so-called 'documentary' or 'anthropological' within the overall narrative. Obviously, Graham Martin's use of 'documentary' implies a very limited notion of the artistic subtlety, the inwardly sympathetic representation provided by the narrator. Obviously, too, a lengthier and more detailed analysis would provide evidence of these features elsewhere in the novel. But my aim has been to establish the *kind* of work we are dealing with, rather than offer a comprehensive account of it. What we have not been able to explore at all, however, is the overall development of events or patterning of the work.

ACTIVITY

Whether or not you agree with Graham Martin's first reading, it should at least be clear that the novel *has* a structure. This is the kind of thing that becomes much more obvious when you re-read a novel. It is in any case evident as soon as you reach Chapter 14, if not before: here is where Part Two begins, as Okonkwo arrives in Mbanta, his mother's village, to which he has been exiled for seven years for the accidental killing of his clansman Ezeudu's young son. Part Three starts with Chapter 20 on page 121.

Now, how, exactly, does this tripartite division work? What is its effect and importance? Does it reveal the separation of the 'documentary' into self-contained stories, as Graham Martin suggests, or does it reveal a more integrated, 'rhythmic' structure? Try summarizing what happens in each part – where the story has taken us, and how it does so – to help you answer.

SAMPLE ANSWER/DISCUSSION

Every reader remembers different things, and so will answer these questions differently. But some things are likely to feature in any account of the three parts. The first part, by far the longest (it is longer than the other two put together), reveals – through a succession of episodes identified in relation to the seasons, clan rituals or ceremonies – various facets of the character of Okonkwo, his family, friends and people. Although what happens to Okonkwo is our main focus, there is a constantly shifting perspective upon the surrounding society and its belief-system. Hence such episodes as the Feast of the New Yam in Chapters 5 and 6, or the judging by the *egwugwu* (ancestor-spirits) of the marriage-dispute in Chapter 10, in both of which Okonkwo is involved. Public and private, material and spiritual, have been shown to be indissolubly integrated, at the same time as the central character's relationship with his society and environment has been elucidated.

The most memorable and important event of this part is the killing of Ikemefuna in Chapter 7. This event is incomprehensible without the context that defines and elaborates its meaning. Simply to read it as a matter of 'recounting' the way in which village quarrels are settled is less than adequate. But there is a sense in which it is not really the climax of Part One, which comes instead at the funeral when Okonkwo's gun explodes, setting in motion the events of the rest of the story: his exile, then return and subsequent downfall; and the break up of the tribe. The latter events, we note, are covered by Parts Two and Three – they could almost be called 'Exile' and 'Return', if that did not place the emphasis too much on Okonkwo. After Part One we know and understand how traditional Igbo society operates, so Parts Two and Three can be correspondingly condensed, covering longer periods of time.

Moreover, the parts are connected by the interweaving of parallels and analogous events so as to provide an accumulating resonance to the story, the *histoire*, which therefore requires less elaboration. The killing of Ezeudu's son not only echoes the earlier killing of Ikemefuna (Ezeudu, we recall, advised Okonkwo not to have a hand in his foster-son's execution), it also foreshadows the violent and self-destructive end of the novel when, once again, Okonkwo acts in defiance of the rules of his tribe, at the same time as he struggles to conserve and protect it.

This juxtaposing linkage of the major events in the novel, I would suggest, becomes more obvious as you proceed through it, as does the speeding-up of the action towards the conclusion. The seven years of Okonkwo's exile in his motherland – the result, ironically for someone so committed to 'male' values, of a 'female' crime against the earth goddess – take up only six chapters. These depict the 'female' side of his life, when he is obliged to be engaged on family affairs, having to suffer and endure rather than go in for his earlier 'masculine' exploits. In Mbanta, the viewpoint shifts noticeably towards the perspective of his wives and children, some of whose names we are given for the first time. The main action at first occurs elsewhere, to be reported to Okonkwo by his friend Obierika (whom we recall as someone more willing to compromise). When Obierika first visits Okonkwo, he tells him of the appearance of a white man in their clan – 'an albino', suggests Okonkwo. The white person has been killed because the Oracle said (truly, of course, on one level) that he 'would break their clan and spread destruction among them' (p.97). Obierika's next visit two years later brings a longer story, to explain the appearance of Okonkwo's son, Nwoye, among the Christian converts in Umuofia; a story that then modulates into an account of the growth of the new religion in Mbanta itself.

Part Three comprises six chapters again, yet seems to move more swiftly, as actions follow one another with greater speed, and without any of the earlier intervening accounts of clan ceremony. The last such 'intervention' (as I've tried to suggest, it may be a misreading to interpret these as less than integral) takes place at the end of Part Two, to which it forms the fitting climax. This is Chapter 19, the great thanksgiving feast for Okonkwo's kinspeople, which concludes with the words of one of the oldest, 'I fear for the clan' and, turning to Okonkwo, 'Thank you for calling us together' (p.118). In short, it is a final assertion of the cohesive traditional values that are threatened by the arrival of the whites.

This arrival was long foreshadowed by the story of the 'lepers' with no toes (i.e. with shoes), when the whites were at a safe distance; now they are in the clan's midst. The different cultures apparently coexist well enough under the first missionary, the tolerant Mr Brown, but the arrival of his more fervent and narrow-minded replacement Mr Smith quickly arouses the potential for conflict in the new and unprecedented (in the clan's history) situation, leading to the destruction of the mission-church (Chapter 22); which, in turn, brings about the arrest and humiliation of Okonkwo and the elders. This leads inevitably to the protest-meeting, the murder of the messenger, and Okonkwo's suicide, followed by the aforementioned concluding chapter.

The structure of a novel is, of course, an abstraction from the words that make it up, its linguistic texture. The impression of a highly organized development such as I have outlined is reinforced if you consider any of the later scenes or chapters in detail, paying attention to its language.

ACTIVITY

Let's take just one example from later in the novel, Chapter 16 in Part Two. What, briefly, happens in it, and how does that relate to the rest of the novel? Look closely at the use of language in it: what is the attitude towards language here, and how (if at all) does it differ from the attitude in earlier chapters?

SAMPLE ANSWER/DISCUSSION

This chapter shows the estrangement between Okonkwo and his son Nwoye, and how this has been brought about by a combination of the father's sternness and the boy's 'vague and persistent' questioning of the tribe's beliefs – a questioning begun by the killing of Ikemefuna (linked as that was to the disposal of twins in the forest), and to which the arrival of Christianity begins to provide some answers. This clearly reinforces our sense throughout of how the private domain is affected by what is happening and has happened in this society and the culture as a whole.

You might have noticed how Nwoye's feelings are expressed in terms of a dryness for which the hymns of the converts offer 'drops of frozen rain' (p.104). There is in fact a gradual depletion of proverbial and Igbo expressions as we enter Parts Two and Three, and the appearance of a more conventionally 'English' discourse as the world of the colonizer imposes itself on the colonized, with one truly barbarous neologism, 'kotma' (for court messenger) signalling the unfortunate corruptibility of the cultural intermediaries who carry out the white man's orders. (Significantly, the word doesn't appear until Chapter 20 in Part Three, p.123.) Here the tensions set up by the arrival of the missionaries are indicated by the white man's first attempt to speak to the people of Mbanta – through an interpreter who, though 'an Ibo man', uses a dialect 'different and harsh' to their ears, including a way of saying 'myself' that means to them 'my buttocks' (p.102). At this stage, the people can afford to make jokes about this. Meanwhile, if the 'mad logic' of the mysteries of the Trinity fails to reach the missionary's audience, 'the poetry of the new religion' does at least appeal to Nwoye, whose viewpoint has already helped to define the weaknesses inherent in pagan belief.

The potential for compromise or at least coexistence between the cultures is present here as it is later, increasingly showing up the alienation of Okonkwo himself from his people, his clan and, ultimately, the movement of history. This is what precipitates his tragedy. The traditional and the Christian cultures can coexist, but not with men like Okonkwo – nor, it is implied, the equally recalcitrant Reverend Smith. The new religion is, however, only part of the new culture. In the opening chapter of Part Three, 'Holy Communion' has become 'Holy Feast' in the tribal language (p.123). But, simultaneously, the law arrives. 'Does the white man understand our custom about land?', Okonkwo then asks Obierika. 'How can he when he does not even speak our tongue?' is the reply, in a speech that continues with a conscious echo of the title:

> 'The white man is very clever. He came quietly and peaceably with his
> religion. We were amused at his foolishness and allowed him to stay. Now
> he has won our brothers, and our clan can no longer act like one. He has
> put a knife on the things that held us together and we have fallen apart.'
> (pp.124–5)

Elsewhere in Nigeria, elsewhere in Africa, conquest *preceded* cultural penetration; Achebe has chosen the less obvious, the more subtle but, as this emphasizes, in the end equally inevitable case.

What this passage also clarifies is the *objectivity* of the novel: the blame for things falling apart is by no means placed only on the arrival of white people, much less on their individual characteristics (Achebe has been criticized for producing caricatures, for example). Rather it is a matter of the forces of destruction being internal as well as external. Achebe's novel gives us full access to the processes of history. (This might prompt a re-reading of the Yeats poem from which the title is taken, by the way, as a view of Irish and British history equally complex: see Said's essay in the Reader, Part One.) And, further, the coming of the whites has meant not only a new life for the outcasts and 'inferior' of the tribe, it has brought increasing prosperity to the whole of Umuofia. This is perhaps the final irony of the novel: we are left with the feeling that, despite the dignity (even grandeur) of the traditional way of life that is so stoutly defended to the end by Okonkwo, he comes to seem a reactionary figure, refusing the challenge of the new world coming into being. There is something sadly appropriate about his death by suicide – 'an abomination' from the traditional point of view, 'an offence against the Earth' (p.147). He has realized that his people cannot, will not, go his way, the way of the past that has been superseded. How do you respond to his death? Do you share Obierika's view of it, 'one of the greatest men in Umuofia' driven by the white man to kill himself and so 'be buried like a dog'? Is it a personal tragedy? Or the clan's? And with what view of the African past are you left?

2.20   How you answer these questions may help you decide how you evaluate the novel's achievement. In my view, you need to take into account the kind of novel you are dealing with, how it asks to be read, as I've tried to suggest. But that doesn't necessarily make the task of judging it any easier. Does it also depend on your 'ideological side'?

ACTIVITY

The phrase comes from Achebe's important essay, 'Colonialist criticism', in the Reader. What position does Achebe himself write from there – when, for example, he remarks that 'A man who does not lick his lips, can he blame the harmattan for drying them?' (Reader, p.279)? If, as this seems to imply, Africans shouldn't complain about the criticisms of Europeans if they're not willing to engage in serious critical evaluation themselves, what does Achebe himself offer?

You will need to read the whole extract, 'Colonialist criticism' (Reader, pp.271–9), to put together an answer. When you have done that, however, there is a further development in the argument to consider. If you have the time, I suggest you read the extract that succeeds Achebe's, by Chinweizu and his colleagues ('Decolonizing African literature', Reader, pp.279–88). In particular, what do you make of the argument that the African novel should be regarded as a narrative form with important indigenous African antecedents (pp.279–85)? Do the 'oral' elements in the narrative of *Things Fall Apart* make us aware that we shouldn't judge it in the familiar terms of Western narrative fiction? If not, then how should we judge it? As a new but 'mixed' genre of writing? Or the inheritor of a 'universal' narrative legacy, as seems to be the answer supplied by Chinweizu *et al.*? You will need to read these extracts carefully before you answer.

2.21   At the least, these essays make us aware of how ethnocentric our own position is; they might also help us to move away from that, towards a better understanding and appreciation of how much the 'new' writers offer us – which is more than just a novel (or a play, a set of poems), although that is a lot; but a new way of looking at literature, at culture, and ourselves.

3   African voices II: 'Madmen and Specialists'

3.1   This section of the block has three aims:

(a)   to help you in your study of *Madmen and Specialists*, the play by the Nigerian writer Wole Soyinka (b.1934);

(b)   to continue discussion of the issue central to the study of drama – the relation between play-texts and play-performances;

(c)   to explore the problem of 'ideology' in relation to one of the new writings in drama.

Before reading any further in this section, you should have first viewed the TV production of *Madmen and Specialists*, which is an edited version of the full play, and also read the play-text. You will come across some Yoruba songs, which can be translated as follows:

Lift, lift us home, Lift
Lift, lift us home, Lift
Palm oil of the farm, mask of
            the road
Lift us home
Lift, lift us home

(p.18)

As it was
So it will be
As it was
So it will be
As it was in the beginning …

(p.40)

As it was
So it will be
As it was
So it will be

(p.71)

As it was
So it will be
So it will be
As it was, was done

(p.77)

The play as 'story'

3.2   You will remember from Block 1 Section 2 ('Drama') that any play can be thought of as a narrative that happens to lack a narrator, using only its characters to convey the story. As in prose fiction, a play's story has narrative momentum pressing forwards towards a conclusion, continually raising and answering the viewer's implicit question, 'what will happen next?' The story is conveyed by what the characters say, how they look, what clothes they wear, their relationships with each other, and what happens between them; and also by the stage-setting, or settings, indicating the place and places where the story is happening, sometimes (as in *Endgame*) offering a kind of mute story of their own.

ACTIVITY

So what story does *Madmen and Specialists* tell? Summarize it as best you can in two or three paragraphs and then, after re-reading the first stage direction about the stage-setting (p.7), consider whether this directly contributes a narrative aspect. Don't read on till you have tried your hand at this exercise.

SAMPLE ANSWER

The characters can be divided into two contrasting sets, those whose home is the village (Si Bero, Iya Agba, Iya Mate, the Priest), and those connected with it, but who have also had experience of the war (Dr Bero who is the brother of Si Bero, the Old Man who is their father, and the Mendicants – Aafaa, Blindman, Goyi and the Cripple – sent to the village by Dr Bero). The play's story has two strands, each associated with one set of characters.

The principal strand concerns the second set of characters, and is mainly about their experience of the war, conveyed indirectly, sometimes even obscurely (much of it not so much told, as alluded to). Dr Bero, originally the doctor in the village, first joined the Medical Corps, then transferred to the Intelligence Section (p.31). The Old Man, after reading a letter about the war from his son, also joined up, undertaking remedial tasks with the wounded, such as the Mendicants to whom he also taught the religion of As. The effect of his son's letter was such that he seriously proposed to the Priest that cannibalism be legalized (p.34). Later, he succeeded in arranging that senior military personnel, including his son, ate a meal of human flesh. Dr Bero then rescued him from the anger of his military superiors, and had him brought to the village by the Mendicants in order to find out the secret meaning of the religion of As. Imprisoned in the surgery, the Old Man gives his son only riddling replies, and is threatened with death. The Mendicants are also ordered to spy on the activities of Si Bero. This narrative strand ends, very puzzlingly it has to be conceded, when the Cripple, attacked by the other Mendicants, is about to be killed by the Old Man, whom Bero then shoots.

The second narrative strand concerns Si Bero, Iya Agba and Iya Mate. The latter are described as 'old Women' (p.6), and they speak for a traditional wisdom, both medicinal and moral. As skilled herbalists, they instruct Si Bero in their age-old practices, having her gather and store the various herbs. They praise her as 'a good woman' (p.16), but denounce her brother as 'evil' (p.75). Though he dismisses them as relics of a superstitious and superannuated culture, he wants to take advantage of their medicinal powers. Suspecting that he will misuse their herbs, they reject Si Bero's pleas on his behalf, and when he shoots the Old Man, they set fire to the store of herbs, which is the play's conclusion.

As to stage-setting, I hope you noticed that there are three distinct acting locations, one above the other. The highest is the 'semi-open hut' (p.7), the domain of Iya Agba and Iya Mate. The lowest, not visible to the audience till Part Two, is the surgery in the cellar where the Old Man is imprisoned. The middle location is the herbal store and the space outside it, the village lane, where we first meet the Mendicants in Part One, where Bero arrives to be greeted by his sister, and has his conversation with the Priest. I suggested that this stage-setting might have its narrative aspect. What I meant was that it establishes a hierarchy for the different events. The hut is the site of traditional wisdom, the surgery the place where modern 'specialists' (both doctors and torturers) are at work, and the middle location is where these two interact. There seems a resemblance to Elizabethan staging practice – heaven above the stage where the main action occurs, and hell below.

DISCUSSION

As with all summaries of a complex narrative, mine doesn't get us very far; and of course other summaries are possible as to detail. But the point of the exercise is to ensure that you have got hold of the play's main drift. In contrast with how we might approach a play such as *Serjeant Musgrave's Dance*, we have to assemble the narrative of *Madmen and Specialists* from details scattered throughout the whole action, often conveyed to us by brief allusions in fast-moving dialogue whose main message is hardly 'narrative' at all. (Contrast the way Musgrave's explanation to his soldiers of what he is about explicitly provides the audience with all essential information.) Thus, when the Mendicants first refer to the religion of As, we might well think it an example of their obscure prattle. Only later do we learn that it is at the very centre of the story, and indeed of the play.

Grasping the main narrative also brings out an important point about the characters. Making the contrast again with *Serjeant Musgrave*, Soyinka's characters are simple, little more than names for particular points of view, whereas Arden provides his main characters with a set of past and motivating experiences, as if in a 'realist' novel, and their specific and varied inter-relationships are essential to the final outcome. Soyinka's characters are hardly explained. They don't have 'relationships' with each other, save of the simplest kind. We know very little about their past – for example, *why* Dr Bero turned from one specialism (medicine and healing) to another (inquisition and torture). The Old Man and the two Mothers take their identities almost entirely from the opinions they hold, and the Mendicants primarily from their war experience. Just as the stage-setting suggests general moral categories, so the characters seem to belong within a moral fable. The play's title carries the same kind of implication, identifying not characters in the 'realist' mould, but issues. Think how different it would be if the title were *Dr Bero's Dance*.

A further point worth stressing is that much the larger proportion of the play's narrative happened before the play itself. What we are actually shown is, from the narrative angle, minimal. (Again, the contrast with Arden's play is instructive.) In Part One, the main events are Dr Bero's return to the village, his orders to the Mendicants, his meetings with the Priest and Si Bero. In Part Two, the main event is Dr Bero's extended confrontation with the Old Man, which ends in the shooting. In both parts the two Mothers are primarily commentators. Their meeting with Dr Bero threatens, but fails to produce, action. Their one decisive act, when they set the herbal store alight, ends the play. So what the play primarily presents is a series of conversations, often puzzling and sometimes really obscure, mainly because they refer to experiences shared by (or at least known to) the speakers, but not directly by the audience. That is another reason why, in studying the play, it is essential to work out this *earlier* narrative content, which gives it some of the character of a detective story whose clues we have to look out for and interpret. But it is also a meditation, an analysis, an anguished probing and evaluation of the characters' past. This invites another contrast with a play you have studied during the course, Beckett's *Endgame*. There, too, verbal exchanges between the characters are all we have. From start to finish, little happens save the comings and goings of Clov. Considered as narrative, *Endgame* is circular, referring to nothing but itself. Soyinka's play, though it shows the influence of Beckett, differs absolutely in this respect. It always refers beyond itself to those experiences that Dr Bero, the Old Man and the Mendicants variously have shared – the war that transformed Bero from doctor to inquisitor and the Old Man into the proponent of the religion of As, and that afflicted the Mendicants with their crushing wounds and disabilities.

The play as 'discourse'

ACTIVITY

Having considered the play in these general ways, I want now to engage more closely with its detail – in effect, with its 'discourse', the ways in which it presents us with the story, the characters and their past experience. Please now re-read Part One as far as the stage-direction (p.23) announcing Bero's entry to the scene. How do the conversation and behaviour of the Mendicants introduce us to their experiences in the war? Do they give us any clues about the play's central theme?

How does the scene in which Iya Mate, Iya Agba and Si Bero appear (pp.16–18) differ in method, and how does it relate to the play as a whole?

Make notes on these points before reading on.

SAMPLE ANSWER

The very appearance of the Mendicants – the visible evidence of their physical sufferings – and the dice game in which the stakes are eyes, arms and the stumps of amputated limbs, of course speak very directly about the war. The fact that they can play such a game implies both stoic acceptance of their mutilated condition and the random character of war wounds, as random as the fall of the dice. Beyond that, however, their cheerful miming of sadistic inquisitions and the parodic representation of official rhetorics (militaristic, racist) bring us close to the play's central concerns. The dramatic method here (mime and parody) suggests that the Mendicants take all this in their stride as, quite simply, how the world works. There is no explicit comment or judgement. Yet the element of *play* – play at tortures, interrogations, executions – brings home to us with horrible vividness the realities they both imitate and mock.

The scene with the two Mothers and Si Bero is different. Clearly it dramatizes a sphere of traditional values – of women faithful to absent husbands, of healing care, of homes to return to, of anxious separation and joyful celebratory greetings, all this in sharp and troubling contrast with the brutal world represented and suggested by the Mendicants. If we keep in mind the specific stage location for these values, their relevance to the play as a whole needs no labouring. But there is a less explicit significance in the Mothers' comments on the rare poison berry that Si Bero has found. She offers to burn it:

IYA MATE Do nothing of the sort. You don't learn good things unless you learn evil.

SI BERO But it's poison.

IYA MATE It grows.

IYA AGBA Rain falls on it.

IYA MATE It sucks the dew.

IYA AGBA It lives.

IYA MATE It dies.

IYA AGBA Same as any other. An-hn, same as any other.

SI BERO That means I still have to find the right one.

IYA AGBA It will be in the same place. They grow together most of the time.

(p.17)

The moral position that the Mothers speak for may be 'traditional', but it is not simple or easy. Good and evil grow together. Their pupil, Si Bero, whom they describe as 'a good woman' (p.16), has still to learn that knowledge of one involves knowledge of the other, though how this relates to the play only becomes clear in Part Two. Notice also how their naturalistic dialogue (see Block 2 Section 9) easily gives way to a different kind of language, the heightened rhythm and poetic suggestiveness of the interchange between the two Mothers in the above quotation. Here, it is as if they speak with one voice, jointly articulating a mysterious wisdom, to which only they have access.

The religion of 'As'

ACTIVITY

Please now re-read the rest of Part One (to p.40). Why does Soyinka interrupt the conversation between Bero and his sister with the brief exchange between the two Mothers (pp.29–30)? What do we learn about Bero's ideas? And what do we learn about the Old Man and the new religion he has been teaching to the Mendicants? Make notes on these points before reading on.

SAMPLE ANSWER

Before brother and sister meet, we already know from Aafa's speech (p.25) that Bero *is* 'a specialist', and we also know what that means – both from the earlier scenes we have just considered, and from Bero's behaviour:

> *Bero cuts him across the face with his swagger stick. Aafaa staggers back, clutching the wound. Bero stands still, watching him. At the sound of pain Iya Agba looks out of the hut and impassively observes the scene.*
>
> (p.26)

But Si Bero knows nothing of all this. She greets her brother with the traditional ritual, pouring palm wine on the ground in front of the house (a ceremony he clearly despises), and asks anxiously of the whereabouts of their father, the Old Man, to which Bero gives only evasive replies. Si Bero then mentions the help she has had from the Old Women, the Mothers, whereupon follows the stage direction (p.28) 'freezing' the brother and sister and introducing the exchange between the Mothers. As I hope you noticed, this abrupt shift of attention underlines their role as commentators and judges of the main action.

What they say develops the enigmatic vein of their earlier remarks about good and evil. They speak of Bero as a seed they have planted, referring presumably to the fact that, as doctor, he was carrying forward into the modern world their immemorial function as healers. Si Bero, too, they have 'planted', and of her they are quite sure:

IYA AGBA   She sucked my head dry.

IYA MATE   She is a good woman.

IYA AGBA   Yes, but what about him?

IYA MATE   You sense something wrong in him?

IYA AGBA   It's my life that's gone into his. I haven't burrowed so deep to cast good earth on worthless seeds.

(p.29)

Bero and his sister are thus conceived as potential inheritors of their traditional wisdom. But how will he turn out? Or rather, how *has* he turned out? This is the question the play goes on to answer.

As if in direct response to the Mothers' exchange, Bero's own ideas are now set out without any possibility of misunderstanding. He has found his 'new vocation' in the Intelligence Section (p.31). He explains to this sisters:

> A laboratory is important. Everything helps. Control, sister, control. Power comes from bending Nature to your will. The Specialist they called me, and a specialist is – well – a specialist. You analyse, you diagnose, you – [*He aims an imaginary gun.*] – prescribe.
>
> (pp.31–2)

Such language directly embodies the effect of the war on Bero. The medical and scientific knowledge that, as a doctor, he had used to heal people, he now uses to control them, and 'control' is, of course, a sinister understatement. Is this a direct allusion to the sort of doctors who, under the Nazi regime, used concentration-camp prisoners as material for experiments into the effect of potentially harmful drugs? There are many other examples of such medical torturers. But it is clear enough that Bero now uses his medical knowledge as a way of exercising power, of 'bending Nature' to his will (equally sinister when we think of its application to human bodies), and of prescribing ... death. He does this in the service of the 'Big Braids' (p.31) – a suggestive phrase (the elaborate decoration on caps and uniforms of senior military personnel, also alluding to Orwell's term for a totalitarian dictator, Big Brother) – but clearly, too, for his own pleasure. Otherwise, how could it be a vocation?

As to his father, the Old Man, we learn that the effect of the war has been very different. The exchange between Bero and the village Priest reveals that the letter from Bero, presumably about his war experiences (whether before or after his move from the Medical Corps to the Intelligence Section is not disclosed), had two intimately connected results. The Old Man proposed to the Priest that cannibalism be legalized, and the next day himself set out to join the Medical Corps (p.34). He put his cannibalism argument into practice (in Part Two we get the full story), and he also expounded a new religion. Bero explains to his sister:

> BERO   ... We thought it was a joke. I'll bless the meat, he said. And then – As Was the Beginning, As is, Now, As Ever shall be ... world without ... We said amen with a straight face and sat down to eat. Then, afterwards ...
>
> SI BERO   Yes?
>
> BERO   He told us. [*Pause. He laughs suddenly.*] But why not? Afterwards I said why not? What is one flesh from another? So I tried it again, just to be sure of myself. It was the first step to power you understand. Power in its purest sense. The end of inhibitions. The conquest of the weakness of your too human flesh with all its sentiment. So again, all to myself I said Amen to his grace.
>
> (p.36)

What exactly is this grace? What religion (if that *is* the term) does it belong to? In teaching it to the Mendicants, what was the Old Man about? From Bero's words, it seems to be a way of validating cannibalism. Soyinka's phrasing alludes to the end of the Creed, the summary of what a member of the Church of England undertakes to believe. As set out in The Book of Common Prayer, this Creed begins:

> Whosoever will be saved: before all things it is necessary that he hold the Catholick Faith.

After listing the key dogma of that faith, it ends:

> Glory be to the Father, and to the Son: and to the Holy Ghost;
>
> As it was in the beginning, is now, and ever shall be: world without end. Amen.

Remembering the Old Man's argument with the village Priest, we can be sure that his adaptation of this liturgical invocation is explicitly sardonic. One central dogma and ritual of Christianity is the act of Holy Communion where, in symbolic form, the body and blood of Christ are consumed by the worshippers. The 'cannibalistic' implications of this are, in effect, spelled out by the Old Man's argument. Within the context of the Christian Creed, 'As it was in the beginning...' affirms the eternal existence of God. What eternal principle is the Old Man affirming? Could it be cannibalism? That seems to be how Bero takes it. 'What is one flesh from another?' he asks, the implication being that, since human beings are carnivores, the taboo on eating each other is mere sentimentality, and to break the taboo is the 'first step to power ... in its purest sense'.

A riddling and enigmatically witty exchange between two Mendicants makes the same point. The Cripple eats a flea he found in his rags.

AAFAA   Did you choose it?

CRIPPLE   It chose me.

BLINDMAN   Chose? An enemy of As.

AAFAA   Sure? Not a disciple.

BLINDMAN   An enemy. Subversive agent.

AAFAA   Quite right. As chooses, man accepts. Had it sucked any blood?

CRIPPLE   It tasted bloody.

GOYI   Accept my sympathies.

CRIPPLE   Not needed. The blood is back where it belongs.

AAFAA   The cycle is complete?

CRIPPLE   Definitely.

> ...

BLINDMAN   That's good. The cycle of As. Tell the Old Man that – he'll be pleased.

(p.39)

The flea sucked the Cripple's blood; the Cripple ate the flea; this completes the 'cycle of As'. The Old Man's recommendation of cannibalism, then, seems to be a way of insisting that *all* animals, humankind included, survive by preying upon each other. (The flea, after all, is not a carnivore.) But Blindman's question, 'Choose? An enemy of As', introduces a complication. 'As chooses, man accepts', comments Aafaa. As physical beings, humankind is locked into the cycle, wholly obedient to it. So to *choose* is to be an enemy, a subversive, a rebel against the deity of As. This helps to explain another thing we learn about the Old Man's relation with the Mendicants. Bero tells his sister:

> Father's assignment was to help the wounded readjust to the pieces and remnants of their bodies. Physically ... Instead he began to teach them to think, think, THINK! Can you picture a more treacherous deed than to place a working mind in a mangled body?
>
> (p.37)

For Bero, to whom the achievement and exercise of power over other human beings are the summit of ambition, teaching people to think for themselves is the most radical of threats. 'A working mind in a mangled body' will lead to questions about the cause of its sufferings, and for the Mendicants that cause was the war in which Bero was transformed from doctor into inquisitor. The Old Man's job was to help the Mendicants to become reconciled to their condition, not to question it. So, for Bero and the system he serves, he is extremely dangerous. We are thus left with a paradox. On the one hand, the Old Man teaches the religion of As, a fatalistic acceptance of the conditions of physical life, a dog-eat-dog philosophy. Yet on the other, he tries to encourage critical thinking, the act of choice, and hence (from the angle of As) subversion and rebellion.

ACTIVITY

One more question before we move to Part Two. Si Bero is present throughout these exchanges. She hears Bero telling the Priest about the pleasure of eating human flesh, at first thinks it a joke (p.35), but then learns that her brother means every word. Her questions about their father elicit Bero's account of the religion of As, and she also hears the Mendicants explain it in their own way. Remembering that she is a disciple of the Old Women, what is to be made of her reactions to all this? Read through pages 35–40, noting her reactions. What view of them do you take?

SAMPLE ANSWER

Her term for Bero's disclosures is 'Abomination' (p.36). Following the Mendicants' exposition of the 'cycle of As', she calls them 'loathsome toads' (p.39). When Bero invites her to see their father, the stage direction reads:

> Si Bero looks at him with increasing horror and disbelief. She turns and runs towards the Old Women who receive her at the door of the hut.
>
> (p.40)

Si Bero, in sum, speaks for an immediate moral rejection of Bero's world. Bero himself reinforces that black-and-white distinction, dismissing her objections, telling her to remain 'in [your little world] … That way you'll be safe' (p.36). So, too, the Mendicants care little for her denunciation.

AAFAA   [grinning] Toads again. You hear that?

CRIPPLE   She was looking at you.

AAFAA   What! I must say I feel insulted.

CRIPPLE   A man must have some pride.

GOYI   My pride is – As.

(p.40)

Two worlds, then – one safe, traditional, of the past; the other dangerous, cruel, modern; each belonging within its distinct narrative strand.

But do we here accept this straightforward moral distinction? Isn't Si Bero's position represented as a flight from an inescapable reality? The Mendicants' sardonic response to her insult undermines its effect. They turn it into yet another joke, parodying simple moral indignation as, in effect, childish. And I find it significant that when it comes to the point, Si Bero rejects the invitation to see her father, as if, like his son, the Old Man now belongs to a world in which she can have no role. The traditional sanctities of family loyalty no longer have power or influence in the world represented by the surgery where Bero (servant of the Big Braids), the Mendicants (in a sense, their victims), and the Old Man are now at last disclosed:

Bero goes on into the clinic where the light has come on, revealing the Old Man seated in the midst of the chanting Mendicants. Lights fade slowly.

And this world is the modern world.

A 'specialist' interrogation

ACTIVITY

In Part Two, the main issues unanswered in Part One – Bero's reason for bringing the Old Man to the village, and exactly what the Old Man has been teaching the Mendicants – are now fully explored. Taking these in order, re-read as far as page 66, making notes on the exchanges between Bero and the Old Man. What does Bero want to find out? What method does he use? Does he succeed? Do we, as audience, learn something that escapes Bero? There is some risk of simplifying the play's effect by my firing off such very specific questions. Still, much of the action proceeds by means of questions, especially in Part Two – an extended interrogation. And as we've seen, the characterization and narrative structure are so designed as to engage general issues. See what answers you come up with before reading on.

SAMPLE ANSWER

Bero wants to find out the secret of the Old Man's influence over the Mendicants, what the religion of As amounts to, and for an evident reason. Since it's a form of power, he wants it for himself. His method is, by implication, the kind parodied by the Mendicants in Part One – inquisition with the threat of torture and/or execution. He doesn't succeed, because in order to grasp the Old Man's ideas he would have to abandon his obsession with power, the basic point that we, as audience, have access to.

DISCUSSION

Bero adopts the cat-and-mouse game that 'specialist' interrogators use on their victims: the refusal to give the Old Man writing paper because he has no money; first letting him have his pipe, then refusing matches; eventually offering cigarettes instead of his pipe; then telling him the food is his 'last meal' (p.51). The overt mildness of this treatment menacingly points to the cruel reality. So, too, Bero's hammering at the questions 'why As?', 'what is As?' (pp.50, 62), evokes the reality that the Mendicants parody in Part One when Aafaa enacts the torture of Goyi, describing himself as 'a Specialist in truth' (p.14). The Old Man's style of reply – mocking or sly back-answers, capping Bero's questions with his own, dangerously teasing him with half-revelations – is the sole form of resistance available to the victim of such inquisition, eventually provoking the violence (p.62) that betrays the inquisitor's failure. (As you'll read later, Soyinka here draws directly on personal experience.)

We, the audience, learn the secret of As, which Bero hears but is unable to take in:

BERO   And the god you worship?

OLD MAN   Abominates humanity – the fleshy part, that is.

BERO   Why As?

OLD MAN   Because Was – Is – Now …

BERO   Don't!

OLD MAN   So you see, I put you all beyond salvation.

BERO   Why As?

OLD MAN   A code. A word.

BERO   Why As?

OLD MAN   It had to be something.

(p.50)

Then, describing the effect on the soldiers to whom he had supplied the meal of human flesh, he recalls:

OLD MAN   Your faces, gentlemen, your faces. You should see your faces. And your mouths are hanging open … All intelligent animals kill only for food, you know, and you are intelligent animals. Eat-eat-eat-eat-eat-Eat!

(p.51)

The Old Man's message here is very direct. War means killing people, and if human beings are simply intelligent animals, why don't they, like other predatory carnivores, eat those they have killed? That is the satirical lesson he aims to drive home to the Big Braids, and to Bero. Bero has already told his sister that the cannibalistic meal had initiated him into the secret of power. But the Old Man's point challenges Bero's: 'Never admit you are a recidivist once you've tasted the favourite food of As' (p.51). The Old Man's god abominates 'the fleshy part' of humanity because it conceives 'the human' as other than the condition of an intelligent animal. The Old Man's advocacy of the religion of As is his way of getting people to accept their shared animal condition as the essential first step to transcending it. That is why the god he worships 'abominates' humanity. Bero's inability to grasp this is clear:

BERO   … What exactly is As, Old Man?

OLD MAN   As?

BERO   You know As, the playword of your convalescents, the pivot of whatever doctrine you used to confuse their minds, your piffling battering ram at the idealism and purpose of this time and history. What is As, Old Man?

OLD MAN   You seem to have described it to your satisfaction.

(p.62)

This answer enrages Bero and prompts his physical attack on the Old Man, half-throttling him with his swagger stick. Evidently, Bero thinks of himself as advancing 'the purpose of this time and history', and though he doesn't explicitly say so, presumably would justify his exercise of power, his passion for 'control', on the grounds that he serves such a purpose. The Old Man hints at this when he tells Bero that he 'harbours illusions' (p.63), the only thrust that puts Bero on the defensive. Earlier, reminding Bero of the cannibalistic meal, he urges him to accept the fact that he is 'contaminated' (p.51) – in other words, that he shares the human condition. But Bero refuses this insight, still supposing that the religion of As will provide him with 'a magic key' (p.62) to a further source of power. In their final exchange, the Old Man directly mocks Bero's other illusion – that he is, or might be, omnipotent:

OLD MAN   That lightning strikes? It could strike you, no?

BERO   Yes.

OLD MAN   *[quiet triumphant smile]* Then you're not omnipotent. You can't do
a flood and you – *[pause]* – can't always dodge lightning. Why do you
ape the non-existent one who can? Why do you ape nothing?

BERO   You tax my patience. Better watch out in future.

OLD MAN   *[quietly]* The future?

BERO   The future, yes. The End ...

OLD MAN   Justifies the meanness.

(p.66)

Notice the pun on 'the end justifies the means', so often the political
rationalization of cruelty and terror. Not surprisingly, it angers Bero, who
issues his last death threat and leaves the room. When he returns (p.77), he
shoots the Old Man.

The Old Man as Socrates?

ACTIVITY

Let's turn now to the other main issue, the Old Man's relationship with the
Mendicants. Whereas in Part One they are Bero's tools (spying on Si Bero,
keeping secret the Old Man's presence in the surgery), in Part Two, even
though they are the Old Man's gaolers, he seems to have reasserted his
influence over them. How successful has the Old Man been in conveying his
ideas? What have been his methods? What specific lessons, if any, has he tried
to convey? You may want to read again the relevant passages from pages
44–66.

SAMPLE ANSWER

It's clear (isn't it?) that the Mendicants have not been ready pupils. The Old
Man's method has been to write satirical songs for them, which they only
partly remember. One special lesson he wants to teach them is 'self-disgust'
(p.55), yet he seems to have failed. The avidity with which they smoke his
cigarette, and gobble up his food (p.52), shows how little they have succeeded
in recognizing, and so escaping from, the domination of As. Nevertheless, the
note of sardonic parody in so many of their exchanges continues to suggest a
kind of critical awareness, especially voiced by Aafaa in his nonsensical litany
for As (pp.41, 52). Also, despite their endless bickering and scrapping, they
stick together, sharing their miserable condition, even conveying a sort of joy
in their rendering of the songs.

DISCUSSION

Clearly, the point of these songs is to encourage in the Mendicants a critical
attitude towards the authorities. The 'Ballad of the State Visit to the Home of
the De-balled' (p.59) attacks the real indifference and pompous self-regard of
the important visitors. The one entitled 'Pro patria mourir' involves an
interesting example both of what they fail to learn and what they do, if in a
muddled way, learn. First they get the title wrong: its correct version is 'Dulce
et Decorum Est Pro Patria Mori', which you'll remember is the title of Owen's
anti-war poem discussed in Block 1 Section 3. 'Pro Patria mourir' mixes up
Latin and French. Then, the Mendicants turn 'decorum' into 'quorum', and
the Old Man scolds their stupidity, but in vain.

OLD MAN   Decorum. Dulce et Decorum ...

MENDICANTS   ... quorum quorum quorum ...

(p.60)

Yet this turns out not just to be invincible ignorance. They suddenly remember the meaning of 'quorum':

BLINDMAN   In ancient Athens they didn't just have a quorum. Everybody was there! That, children, was democracy.

CRIPPLE   [singing, to the tune of 'When the Saints']

Before I join
The saints above
Before I join
The saints above
I want to sit on that damned quorum
Before I join the saints above.

(p.60)

And the others join in, 'drumming on the floor, table, etc., with their crutches, knuckles, etc., repeating the chorus'. Here, the Old Man has scored a success. They have remembered what he told them about Athenian democracy, and also that 'a quorum' is an aspect of democratic procedure: no decisions are valid without the presence of an adequate number of those with the right to take them. We can be sure that this is the kind of thing the Old Man has been teaching them because Bero enters at this point, and remarks 'So you haven't given up your little tricks'.

Notice that it is Blindman who remembers the point about Athenian democracy, and he is given the long, satirical speech that concludes the Mendicants' parody version of 'royalty visits' (p.69), weaving together racist and imperialist prejudices about 'inferior' peoples, in the style of the archetypal political demagogue:

Rape is more natural to them than marriage. Even Confucius said it – if it must be, lie back and enjoy it. That coming from their greatest – er – er – atomic scientist is not a statement to be taken lightly. The black menace is no figment of my father's imagination. Look here ... have you had the experience of watching them – breed? ... What we have, we hold. What though the wind of change is blowing over this entire continent, our principles and traditions – yes, must be maintained.

(p.70)

The speech combines a kind of lunatic wildness with deep-rooted racist contempt. Notice, too, the stage direction that precedes it: 'the speech should be varied with the topicality and locale of the time' (p.69). That it is the product of the Old Man's teaching is underlined when Blindman, applauded by the others, gains the Old Man's praise: '...It was quite a good effort ... Very much like old times' (p.71).

ACTIVITY

Bero's original accusation about the Old Man was that he had taught the Mendicants 'to think', and we now have a clearer sense of what this amounted to. Are we then to characterize the Old Man as the voice of sanity, reason and democratic human values? Please now re-read from the bottom of page 56 to page 58, during which the two Mothers talk to Bero; and then look at what Bero says to the Old Man on page 61. What view of the Old Man emerges from these pages? Do you notice anything his ideas have in common with those of the Mothers?

SAMPLE ANSWER

We get two views of the Old Man. The Mothers offer to help Bero cure him, having heard that he was 'sick' (p.57). Yet there is a possible connection between their belief and the Old Man's thought. Bero asks them what their cult is:

> IYA AGBA   Not any cult you can destroy. We move as the Earth moves, nothing more. We age as Earth ages.
>
> (p.57)

And when Bero says he will proscribe them, the reply comes:

> IYA AGBA   What can that mean? You'll proscribe Earth itself? How does one do that?
>
> (p.58)

This is not unlike the Old Man's taunt that Bero cannot raise a flood, or escape the possibility of being struck down by lightning. Like the Mothers, he here seems to appeal to non-human powers to which even Bero must bow. The other view of the Old Man is different. Bero gives him some berries he picked up from the herbal store:

> BERO   ... I brought you some. [*He brings some berries from his pockets and drops them gently over the Old Man's head.*] If you ever get tired and you feel you need a nightcap like a certain ancient Greek you were so fond of quoting, just soak a handful of them in water.
>
> (p.61)

The allusion is to Socrates, and to the hemlock he took, having been condemned to death by the state for corrupting the minds of the young – in effect, teaching them to think. Socrates' method was to ask questions, to make his listeners analyse for themselves the grounds of their beliefs. So is the Old Man's method, and this does support the view emerging from his relationship with the Mendicants that the Old Man speaks for sanity and reason. On the other hand, the question remains: is he not also 'sick'? Or are the Mothers just citing hearsay, perhaps from Si Bero? In their exchange with Bero, it is after all *his* sickness that is more evident. Here, as elsewhere, what they say has an oracular ambiguity.

How does the play end?

ACTIVITY

The main reason for asking those questions about the Old Man lies in the play's conclusion, to which we can now turn. Re-read from page 71 to the end. What do you make of the Old Man's behaviour? How does it fit with what we already know about him? How do you view his last act?

DISCUSSION

The situation is too fraught with contradictions to permit an 'answer' to these questions. The Old Man's speech (pp.71–2) expounds As in terms different from those we have so far met. As is now a whole System encompassing all aspects of modern life – political, scientific, metaphysical, economic and ethical – and no one can escape it. The System has an all-powerful priesthood, whose members will deny any shared humanity with the Mendicants, and judge any such claims as *heresy*. Given the Old Man's function as a Socrates of his time and place, we surely have to understand this as satirical mimicry of the priesthood of the System. Aafaa follows on with a comparable denunciation of heretics:

> Oh, look at him, Monsieur l'homme sapiens, look at the lone usurper of the ancient rights and privileges of the priesthood [*The Cripple makes an obscene gesture. Aafaa registers shock.*], look at the dog in dogma raising his hindquarters to cast the scent of his individuality on the lamp-post of Destiny! On him practise, Practise! Practise! As was the Beginning –

MENDICANTS   Practise …

AAFAA   As Is …

MENDICANTS   Practise …

(p.73)

But is *this* a satire on the System, on the priesthood of As that denounces all questioning heretics? Perhaps. Yet the Old Man appears to endorse it, literally and not satirically (p.74), and Aafaa's shocked reaction to the Cripple's obscene gesture against 'priesthood' suggests that he believes what he is saying.

The next scene shows Iya Agba telling Si Bero that her brother is 'carrion. I leave him to earth's rejection' (p.74), and preparing to burn down the herbal store, after which we return to the Old Man in a speech that fully endorses Aafaa's anathema on heretics. The Cripple then intervenes with 'I have a question' (p.76). This identifies him as a 'heretic', an example of 'Monsieur l'homme sapiens'. In swift confirmation, the Mendicants attack him (chorusing 'Practise'), encouraged by the Old Man who suddenly takes on the garb of a specialist (a surgeon), crying:

> Lay him out. Stretch him flat. Strip him bare. Bare! Bare! Bare his soul! Light the stove! … Let us taste just what makes a heretic tick.

(p.77)

Here, the Old Man adopts the role of a priest of As 'practising' on heretics. How can this be reconciled with the earlier episodes that represent him as a latter-day Socrates? The Mothers have suggested that he is sick. Is this the explanation? Has his experience in the war, trying to get the Mendicants to think, arranging the cannibalistic meal for the Big Braids, followed by the long inquisition by his son, turned his mind? Or should we understand the attack on the Cripple as a satiric dramatization of what the System of As necessarily leads to? The Old Man would then be acting out a point of view to which he is absolutely hostile, as if to say: 'here is what devotion to As really means.' Yet another possibility links the Old Man's action with his recommendation of cannibalism. Societies that practised cannibalism believed that by eating the flesh of a brave enemy, his courage and strength would become yours. The Old Man has, in effect, been promoting 'heresy'. Is he here intending that the other Mendicants (who, unlike the Cripple, have not asked 'a question') might develop heretical power by feasting on an actual heretic?

The fact remains that Bero shoots the Old Man, the play ends, and we have no certain way of deciding between these possibilities. Only one thing is sure: the Mothers finally enact their judgement on Bero and everything about the modern world that he stands for.

Genesis and context

3.3   Having now considered *Madmen and Specialists* in detail, we are in a position to explore the question of its 'ideology'. But first, it is necessary to sketch in the context and sources of its genesis.

3.4   Wole Soyinka was born in 1934 in Western Nigeria. His family and culture belonged to Yoruba-speaking peoples. After primary school in his home village, Abeokuta, he attended one of the leading secondary schools of Nigeria in Ibadan, then the capital of the Western Region. In 1952 he was admitted to Ibadan College (then an offshoot of the University of London), one of whose students was Chinua Achebe. Since the college selected its students from all over Nigeria, entry was highly competitive. After two years Soyinka proceeded to the University of Leeds, where he completed an honours degree in English literature in 1957, and during his third year began to write for the stage. From Leeds he moved to London, earned a living as a supply-teacher, and completed his first two plays. In the autumn of 1958 he worked for the Royal Court Theatre, London, as a script-reader, and gained experience of stage-management and direction. This was the period when the Court Theatre was the centre of the revival of British drama during the 1950s. The early plays of John Arden, John Osborne, Arnold Wesker, as well as Samuel Beckett's *Waiting for Godot*, were produced there. Meanwhile, Soyinka's dramatic career in Nigeria started with the production of *The Swamp Dwellers* and *The Lion and the Jewel* at the Arts Theatre, Ibadan, in February 1959.

3.5   In the following year Soyinka was awarded a research fellowship by the Rockefeller Foundation to enable him to explore traditional Nigerian festivals, rituals and masquerades. The Nigeria to which he returned early in 1960 was on the brink of political independence, and Soyinka's next play, *A Dance of the Forests*, was produced in time to celebrate that event on 1 October 1960. It was an elaborate production, which interwove singing, dancing and masquerade with a poetic verbal texture drawing on the myths and legends of Yoruba culture. Its success announced that Soyinka was already a playwright of major importance.

3.6   During the next few years, Soyinka wrote several more plays, a novel *The Interpreters* (1965), and a volume of poems, *Idanre and Other Poems* (1967), and as a director of plays, and sometimes an actor, richly contributed to the developing cultural life of Nigeria. From early in 1966, however, there developed a train of political catastrophes that finally issued in the attempt at secession by the Eastern Region of Nigeria as the independent state of Biafra, an event immediately provoked by a general massacre of Easterners of Ibo origin resident in the Northern Region. Civil war followed. Soyinka took a public anti-war stand which led to his arrest in August 1967 on suspicion of being pro-Biafran, and though no formal charge was ever preferred against him, he remained in prison, much of the time in solitary confinement, till September 1969. In 1972 he published a prose account of this experience, *The Man Died: prison notes*, and a related poem *The Shuttle in the Crypt* (1972). *Madmen and Specialists* (1971) and a second novel, *Season of Anomy* (1973), both draw on his experience of imprisonment, the calamitous civil war and the massacre and widespread arrest of thousands of innocent people as a consequence of the political crisis and severe inter-regional conflicts.

3.7   Here is an extract from the opening sections of *The Man Died*, recounting Soyinka's initial interrogation. Shortly after his arrest, his legs had been chained together:

> Evening. 'E' Branch was overcrowded. Every office, the library, even some landings were used as interrogation rooms. All through the day Ibos and suspected sympathizers were brought in by the hundreds. Denunciation was easy and old scores were settled by a whisper to the police. Some, mostly non-Ibos, came in already defeated by terror, prostrating, pleading for a chance to make a defence. All evening I heard voices of new arrivals, men and women. The words were monotonous, the protests and counter-accusations: 'I never said so. Na lie, I no say dat kin' ting.' It was enough to accuse a man for expressing Ibo sympathy or damning the Army. Or telling the truth of a torture or murder which he had witnessed. It was sufficient to look disapproving on methods of terror.

Night. A weird, brief encounter. I had dozed off. Suddenly the door was flung open and a woman catapulted in. 'Stay there and shut up.' The officer gave orders for some others to be shut away in different offices. From her accent I knew she was Ibo. I had never witnessed such terror in a woman. It was some time before she was even aware that there was another being in the room. The shock – she was at first convinced that it was an officer, perhaps her appointed torturer – the shock took her to the opposite corner of the room from where she stared with huge panicked eyes and a quivering throat which barely stopped short of a shriek. Then her eyes came downwards and she saw the chains. I saw her body go lax, sympathetic. She came forward, her hand patting the table as if to engage some reassurance of concrete things. I watched her silently. She needed no further comforting from me; the sight of my chains had done more than words could have done for her, calmed her down. But then I saw yet a new change in her face. She stood suddenly still, unbelieving. Recognition. I saw it even before she spoke. Are you not … are you not Wole Soyinka? I nodded. From my face, to my legs, back to my face. A pause to take it in. Then she broke down in tears.

The guard – he must have gone off briefly to help with the new influx – looked in a minute and gasped. What is she doing here? He screamed down the corridor for the officer on duty. No one is supposed to go in the room with that suspect! When they all rushed in she had stopped crying. The duty officer was all regretful; he had not known there was anyone in there. They led the woman away, calmer, stronger. She turned round at the door, looked at me in a way to ensure that I saw it, that I knew she was no longer cowed, that nothing ever again would terrorize her. I acknowledged the gesture. I wondered if she knew what strength I drew from the encounter.

D. returned late the following morning. 'Why are you on hunger strike?'

'I am not on hunger strike.'

'No?' He looked puzzled. 'I was told you did not eat last night and you haven't eaten this morning.'

'Oh that! I've been misinterpreted. It's not a hunger strike at all.'

His immediate concern was touching. 'What's the matter? Are you ill?'

'No, I'm very well. Just a simple precautionary measure that's all.'

Outraged now: 'You are afraid of being poisoned.'

'If only you'd let me explain. It's these chains – oh not that I mind them – they are quite comfortable sitting down. Unfortunately going to the lavatory is one walk a man can't avoid taking. I avoid that you see, or minimize it, by not eating.'

'You can't do completely without eating.'

I pointed to the glass of water on the table. 'Just one of that a day. Quite sufficient. By tomorrow I should need to piss only once a day. After that maybe I won't need to go at all. The statement is on the table.'

He took my notes and went out. 'I'll see what can be done.'

Nothing that day. The chains stayed on the second night running. The third morning D. came in to ask some questions – so he said. He came in smiling. 'I hope you've begun eating now.'

'No. The situation has not changed.'

He looked down, saw or pretended to see the chains for the first time. Angry or anger-feigning he summoned the guard and demanded why they had not been removed. The guard explained that he had had no instructions.

'Go and fetch the keys and remove them at once!'

The guard disappeared.

'Sorry about this, Wole' – yes, it became Wole from this morning – 'I gave instructions about them last night. As soon as they have been removed and you've had something to eat I would like us to have another chat. I shall send someone for you.' The chains were removed but I had already passed that crucial stage which I like to refer to as the Battle of the Belly Bugs. Once that pinching feeling is past, fasting turns to floating. The exercise kept me evenly disposed, phlegmatic – I resolved to continue on a lower key, drinking a watered-down tin of milk a day. The guard sent someone to fetch it.

I never had the milk. An hour later D. stormed in, angry.

'How is it that the foreign papers are already carrying news of your arrest?'

I stared blankly. What was that to me?

'How could they have known and why all this publicity? They are already insinuating that you are being ill-treated. I hope you realize that all this publicity is not helping your case one bit. They simply make your position more awkward.'

'What case and what position precisely? If I am innocent of whatever you suspect me of, just what difference should foreign or local publicity make? Or are you now admitting that you presume me guilty already?'

'We are not presuming you anything...'

'Listen, I am not unknown. Even faceless burglars have the event of their arrest publicized. Are you claiming special privileges for the Nigerian Gestapo?'

'Nobody is claiming anything.'

Either he did not hear or had decided to ignore the Gestapo label. Control ... control ... He too seemed to be offering himself the same advice.

'Look Wole, we know you are a world-famous figure, but these foreign papers are naturally mischievous. Any opportunity to slander the authorities...'

Young, intense, uncertain and a victim of the dilemmas of his position, he continued to talk himself out of his unreasonableness. He had after all charged into the room in a tone of accusation and condemnation. And breathing a kind of blackmail.

'I don't really know what you expect me to do,' I complained. 'I can't go out and talk to them. Of course you could always arrange a press conference and produce me...'

An hour later he gave orders that I was to be transferred to Kiri-kiri Prison.

(Soyinka, 1985, pp.42–5)

3.8 As well as illustrating the personal experiences out of which the play was written, there are a couple of sentences that point to one key issue. Did you notice them? If not, work through the extract again. You will find my comment at the end of the section.

The ideology of the play

3.9 We can now take up the issue of the play's 'ideology'. In his discussion of African writing, Soyinka makes a sharp distinction between European and African art. The quest for a 'literary ideology', he proposes, reflects the preoccupation, not of the writer or artist, but of the critic. Moreover:

> The idea of literature as an objective existence in itself is a very European idea, and ideologies are very much systems of thought or speculative goals considered desirable for the health of existing institutions (society, ecology, economic life, etc.) ...
>
> (Reader, p.297)

3.10 He goes on to describe Beckett's struggle 'towards the theatrical
statement that can be made in one word' (ibid., p.298) as an aspect of the
Modernist separation of art from the human life it claims to reflect or
represent. Soyinka's earliest plays, rooted as they are in the beliefs and
practices of Yoruba culture, clearly illustrate his anti-Modernist argument.
Madmen and Specialists, however, differs from these earlier plays. The Yoruba
inheritance is present only in the role of the two Mothers. One critic of
Soyinka's work notes that

> since his emergence from Kaduna jail [it] has been predominantly allegorical
> and generalized in treatment ... neither countries, historical events nor
> individuals are precisely identified in *Madmen and Specialists* or in *Season of
> Anomy*.
>
> (Moore, 1978, p.104)

ACTIVITY

As we have seen, the play is in the form of a moral fable, examining general
issues that (though Soyinka's immediate source was the specific experience of
the Nigerian Civil War) have a relevance to twentieth-century life in all too
many countries of the world. Can it, in that case, be said to propose an
'ideology'? Think back to the detailed discussion of the text, and formulate
your view before reading on.

DISCUSSION

It seems to me that there are two distinct issues here, one related to drama as
an artistic form very different from prose fiction or poetry, the other related
to Soyinka's play.

Drama differs from fiction or poetry because the play-text constitutes only one
element in the total effect of a performance. You will recall, in connection
with Block 1 Section 2 ('Drama'), a related extract in the Reader – Martin
Esslin's 'The signs of drama'. From the angle of semiotics, he argues that any
performance involves the interaction of several distinct sign-systems: words,
staging, the costume and appearance of the actors, the actors' movements, the
scenery (and to this we can add the play-director's particular interpretation of
the written text). For this reason, a play's 'ideology' is always more fluid and
indeterminate than that of the relatively stable texts of prose fiction and
poetry. There the principal variable factor is the historical and cultural
position that the reader brings to the act of interpretation – or, to use the term
to which you were introduced by Roger Day in Block 3, the reader's
'interpretive community'.

This factor is of course also present for the audience of a play. But the further
contributions of specific actors, specific staging and scenery – essential to the
performance of a play-text – mean that its 'ideology' is, within certain limits
imposed by the text, capable of much variation. (The most familiar illustration
is the successive interpretations of Shakespeare's history plays – for example,
the difference between the Olivier wartime film version of *Henry V* and that
of Kenneth Branagh which insists, as Olivier's did not, on the brutality of
hand-to-hand fighting.) In the TV production of *Madmen*, the Mendicants were
not all Nigerian, and Goyi speaks with a recognizably Liverpudlian accent, in
order to bring out the fact that the play's theme is not confined simply to
Nigeria. The Mendicants' wounded state could be a product of any war,
anywhere in the world, and not just in an African state. Another example can
be taken from the TV production of *Endgame*. Hamm is 'black', the other three
actors are 'white'; Clov's and Nell's speech is clearly Irish, Nagg's Cockney,
and Hamm's Guyanan. Again, the intention was to 'universalize' the play's
effect.

As to *Madmen and Specialists*, does it express an 'ideology'? We have seen from its title, staging and structure that the play explicitly addresses general issues, and its content is, in effect, a series of debates. The staging builds in a direct opposition between the attitudes and ideas of the two Mothers on the one hand, and of Bero on the other. Bero is in direct opposition to the Old Man. The Old Man's ideas oppose those of the Priest, and are themselves complex, even contradictory. The religion of As, in his view, should replace Christianity, yet those who adopt it must then question it, must become 'heretics'. Being himself a Socratic questioner of fundamental beliefs, the Old Man seems to represent 'Monsieur l'homme sapiens' (as Aafaa puts it in his muddled way). We have seen that deep contradictions and implicit ideological conflicts characterize several of the A319 texts. What is clear about *Madmen* is the degree to which it brings such conflicts into the open, and leaves their contradictions unresolved. As a literary form, drama is better able to adopt this dialogic method than most prose fiction or poetry, but few plays exploit the method as thoroughly as *Madmen*.

ACTIVITY

Nevertheless, is it possible to say that the play *inclines towards* a particular 'ideology', a preference between the various positions adopted by the characters? Does any one of its ideological voices dominate the others? Does it positively recommend the religion of As? Or some other point of view?

DISCUSSION

Taking first the Old Man's thinking, is it not the case that Soyinka aims here at shocking his audience, as distinct from persuading them? Isn't the point of the Old Man's advocacy of the religion of As to press home the fact that the human species is, like many others, predatory? We survive, physically, by consuming other species. The first human societies lived primarily by hunting other animals. But unlike other mammals, human beings are especially savage towards other human beings. No other species wars against its own kind, or takes pleasure in inflicting pain on its own members. The Old Man's argument for cannibalism seems to be directed against this aimless killing. Other species kill for food, so – he sardonically argues – if you kill, why not eat what you kill? The play presses the question, and leaves its audience to work out an answer. Again, remembering the Old Man in his role as questioner, why does he teach the Mendicants satirical songs? And why does his debate with Bero so often take the form of what might at first seem to be evasive quibbling and word-play? For example, following the episode when Bero gives the Old Man the poison berries, and suggestively alludes to the fate of Socrates, there is this exchange:

> OLD MAN   You've used [the berries] before, haven't you? Or something similar. I saw your victims, afterwards.
>
> BERO   They were provided a Creed but they talked heresy. Same as you.
>
> OLD MAN   Creed? Heresy? Bread, pleurisy and what next? Will you try and speak some intelligible language.
>
> (p.61)

For Bero's abstract concepts the Old Man substitutes words relating to familiar human needs (food, health). He attacks abstractions that Bero, and such as Bero (for example, the Priesthood later referred to in Aafaa's final speech, p.73), use to justify their exercise of power over their victims. The 'Ballad of the State Visit to the Home of the De- balled', in its title as well as in the chorus sung by the Mendicants, satirizes the very notion of a state visit. Such a speech as Blindman's (pp.69–71) composed of powerfully emotive scraps of language, strung together in a more or less random manner, is a satirical version of the use of language not to communicate ideas, but to disguise motives, not to clarify but to conceal. The play has many examples of mocking *parody* of various kinds of language, as if its misuse was one of the corruptions endemic in the modern world. We can from this point of view consider the play's conclusion as the parody of a religious use of language (the denunciatory sermon, the chants, the hypnotic effect of a litany) to validate 'practising' on heretics. In that respect, the tone and tenor of the play are such as to undermine the validity of any of the ideologies it offers for debate, each of which generates its particular language.

There is, however, one point of view, that of the Mothers, which is not subjected to mocking caricature; and as we've seen, their language is economic, tending to brief poetic evocations and, where mysterious, making no effort to disguise the fact. Moreover, as the final judges of Bero and his world, their ideas have a different status from those of the Old Man. They also speak on behalf of the Earth, of chthonic powers and potentialities beyond the reach of human control, and which human societies need to respect. As symbolized in the herbal store, these powers can be used for evil purposes: that is why the Mothers deny the herbal store to Bero. In a striking metaphor, Iya Agba refers to the store as actually being her 'head' (p.75). Does this mean that the play affirms without qualification the pre-modern culture represented by the Mothers? Perhaps. Yet they have their forward-looking aspect. They tell us that Bero and Si Bero are seeds that they have planted, one of which turns out well, the other badly. One implication of this 'twinning' is that Si Bero illustrates a good use of their inherited wisdom. But her character and role are left underdeveloped and, significantly, she never enters the surgery. Is this because her 'goodness' cannot be affirmed in the world as represented by the surgery? The play leaves this question unanswered, and also leaves unexplored whether or not Si Bero, as the good seed, represents a positive *modern* alternative to her brother. For these reasons, the Mothers' ideological position does not seem to me to be *actively* affirmed by the play's conclusion. Si Bero, as their modern representative, stands only for a beneficial possibility that the play leaves unfulfilled.

I will leave you to ponder whether this represents an aspect of the play that Soyinka fails to clarify, or whether, as with the ideas of the Old Man, he intends it as yet another question for his audience to find answers to.

3.11 In paragraph 3.8, I asked you to pick out two sentences from *The Man Died: prison notes* that point to one key issue of the play. What I had in mind is 'Either he did not hear or had decided to ignore the Gestapo label. Control…'

4 Caribbean voices I:
Derek Walcott and Grace Nichols

Introduction

4.1 This section necessarily contains a great deal of contextual information – about the Caribbean islands, about the linguistic situation there, and about the two writers we have chosen to study. It's important, therefore, that before we proceed, you consider the direct, unmediated impact of some poetry.

ACTIVITY

Could you now read Sections 6, 7 and 8 of Derek Walcott's 'The Schooner *Flight*' (in the Poetry Anthology). All you need to know at this stage is that the 'speaker' is a Caribbean seaman. As you are reading, please consider the following:

(a) What 'levels' and types of language are used?

(b) How would you 'place' this verse relative to poets you have already studied for this course? In other words, of whose work does it remind you?

DISCUSSION

(a) There's a difference, isn't there, between the broad 'vernacular' speech in Section 8 (also hinted at in the opening to Section 6) and the stately, meditative, 'high' diction used elsewhere? The last line of Section 6, for instance ('by careful mimicry might become men'), and 'Some case is for fist' in Section 8, come from differing 'worlds' of human experience.

(b) Many answers are possible. The density of Section 6 might, for instance, have reminded you of Geoffrey Hill (though I shall be suggesting that it deliberately echoes Edward Thomas). The use of vernacular might have put you in mind of Tony Harrison. But what strikes me – the point I want to stress – is that this verse is both eminently 'traditional', the product of a writer skilled in 'traditional' metrics and at ease with 'standard English', and very fresh. It is both 'English' and very 'un-English'. The romantic ardour of Section 7, for instance, seems to me closer in spirit to Yeats and Sorley MacLean than to most recent verse from England.

You will discover, though, as you read on, that Walcott has attracted strong, even bitter, criticism for turning away from his native Caribbean heritage and accepting European canons in literature and art. His use of Caribbean vernacular may have struck you as 'radical'; but other Caribbean poets have gone much further in this respect. His verse-rhythms may seem agreeably light and flexible – but, unlike those of certain rival writers, they don't generally spring from Caribbean popular culture. Later you'll be considering a very different Caribbean poet, Grace Nichols. Try to keep open in your mind the possibility that Walcott's methods of writing, complexly resonant with the 'English' or 'European' tradition, may be less valid, less appropriate, for a Caribbean context than hers.

AUDIO-CASSETTE

At this point you could usefully listen for the first time to Audio-cassette 3 Side 2, 'Walcott's "The Schooner *Flight*"'.

4.2   This is the only section of Block 6 concerned with poetry. It is worth pausing to ask to what extent this reflects the 'balance of power', between literary forms, in the 'new writings' in English, and why our chosen poets should be Caribbean.

4.3   The answer to the first question is that prose fiction has in fact been the dominant medium in the new writings. In India, Malaysia and most of Africa, the remoteness of verse in English from the common life is enhanced by its existence in a language that most of the population can't read. This is not to say that it has no social significance. In Malawi, the authorities imprisoned without trial the country's leading English-language poet, Jack Mapanje, in 1987, because of the alleged subversiveness of his writing. During the Nigerian civil war, the elegant Modernist poet Christopher Okigbo died fighting for Biafra. In South Africa, much 'protest poetry' in English has come from the black townships, some of it – Mongane Wally Serote's, for instance – of high quality. But, in answer to the second question, one reason for looking at Caribbean verse in this block could be this: while prose fiction dominates Caribbean literature, poetry nevertheless looms far larger, relatively speaking, than elsewhere in the English-speaking world.

4.4   Creole languages based on European ones are the common speech of the region. Popular culture uses creole in forms – such as calypso and reggae lyrics – that have roots in a singular fusion of European and African influences. West Indian (and 'black British') dub poets are literary artists working in a popular medium that involves music and performance. And popular forms have provided sites for the declaration of political resistance and cultural identity. Poets starting from 'English tradition' or 'Modernism' have had to relate to a potent popular culture. (All this you will be able to see exemplified in TV11 *Caribbean Poetry*.) The result has been a degree of 'newness' to match Achebe's handling of the novel form – newness of form as well as newness of content, a spectacular breach in the Berlin Wall of English canonization.

4.5   Language is a very important and complicated factor in all this. David Dabydeen (who appears in TV11), Guyanese of Asian origin, published in 1984 a first collection of poems, *Slave Song*, in Guyanese creole. He tells us that, having been educated in England, he was ignorant of the creole poetry from the West Indies that already existed. His inspiration came from the medieval *English* poem *Sir Gawain and the Green Knight*, written in an alliterative form in a North of England dialect:

> The sheer naked energy and brutality of the language ... reminded me immediately of the creole of my childhood. John of Trevisa ... [1326–1412] described the alliterative poetry of the North of England as 'harsh, piercing and formless'. This quality of lawlessness and the primarily oral form of delivery bore curious resemblance to Guyanese creole. I began to see, albeit naïvely, the ancient divide between north and south in Britain, the Gawain poet standing in opposition to Chaucer, in terms of native idiom versus an educated, relaxed poetic line tending towards the form of the iambic pentameter. The north/south divide is of course evocative of the divide between the so-called Caribbean periphery and the metropolitan centre of London. London is supposed to provide the models of standard English and we in the Caribbean our dialect versions.
>
> (Dabydeen, 1989, p.181)

You'll see how Dabydeen could relate his own preoccupations to those of Tony Harrison's 'School of Eloquence' sonnets and Tom Leonard's Glaswegian verse, discussed in Block 5. But there is (as Dabydeen himself would emphasize) a point where the analogy breaks down. Harrison and Leonard are not blacks, not 'niggers'. If the former chose to present himself as a classically trained scholar married to an opera singer, the latter as a lover of classical music with an erudite appreciation of nineteenth-century English verse (these are partially true descriptions of these men), 'metropolitan' persons wouldn't doubt their credentials. But black people, being black, aren't readily thought of as being lovers of ancient Greek poetry or Post-Impressionist French art. They are subject in Britain to condescension, contempt, insult and violence. Racism and thuggery, Dabydeen argues,

> force black writers [in Britain] into poetry that is disturbing and passionate. The play of the light of memory upon pine furniture, touching vignettes of domestic life, elegiac recollections of dead relatives, wonderment at the zigzag fall of an autumn leaf, none of these typical English concerns are of special relevance to them. They participate in a West Indian tradition which seeks to subvert English canons by the use of lived nigger themes in lived nigger language.
>
> (Ibid., pp.188–9)

What, then, is this subversive West Indian tradition? We need to look first at the history from which it springs.

A creole literature?

4.6   From Columbus's accidental landfall in the Bahamas in 1492 followed centuries of violence and oppression in the beautiful and fertile Caribbean region. Of the original 'Indian' inhabitants, the Arawaks were virtually exterminated within a couple of centuries, the fiercer Caribs were reduced to small pockets of occupation. The 'Indians' survive, in a ghostly way, in the English language, both standard and creole – 'Caribbean', 'cannibal', 'barbecue', 'hurricane'. But their inability to resist European diseases, or supply the labour needs of white conquerors, meant that immigrants, white and black, would provide the main stock of the islands' population.

4.7   Inspired by Portuguese success in the cultivation of sugar in Brazil, other Europeans began, in the seventeenth century, to occupy the Caribbean archipelago. Dutch, French and English vied for scraps of island, and for the mainland territory of 'Guiana'. At first 'indentured servants' were brought from England, Wales, Scotland and Ireland to work as virtual slaves (though for fixed terms) in the new sugar plantations. But increasingly, as the century wore on, planters drew on the trade in African slaves to the New World, established long before by the Spaniards and Portuguese but eventually dominated by the British.

4.8   An immense amount of scholarship has been devoted in the last half century to the slave-trade, and to conditions in the West Indies, raising many controversial issues. But these broad facts seem beyond dispute:

(a)   Millions of Africans were transported to the New World between the sixteenth and nineteenth centuries. They provided the main population-base of the Caribbean in particular.

(b)   Almost all came from Western Africa, from Mauretania down to Angola. But they varied enormously between themselves in language and customs.

(c)   Typically, an English trader would sail to the Guinea Coast with manufactured goods of a crude kind. He would exchange these for slaves brought to the coast by African 'middlemen'. In addition to those captured during war, Africans were kidnapped for sale by other Africans. The 'middle passage', the voyage from Africa to the Caribbean, was fraught with brutality and disease. Of those who survived, most endured savage discipline in the sugar industry.

(d)   In the British Empire, the trade in slaves was abolished in 1807, slavery itself by 1838. In the age of the industrial revolution, these gestures represented the relative decline of the once powerful 'sugar interest' compared to new fields of capitalist endeavour: the returns from slavery no longer balanced the moral opprobrium attached to it. However, the sugar industry still needed ultra-cheap labour. This was supplied, in Trinidad and Guyana, by the importation of vast numbers of 'indentured' workers from the Indian subcontinent.

(e) Hence by the twentieth century, Caribbean cultures exhibited a range of syntheses of very disparate elements: Iberian, French, Dutch, English and Celtic; African customs and languages as different as those of the Mandingo and the Igbo; and Hindu ways of life from Asia.

4.9 One further factor should be stressed. The term 'creole' historically refers to all people, black and white, actually born in the Caribbean; it contrasts with 'visitor' or 'immigrant'. Within the creole, *native* societies of the Caribbean, a complex colour-snobbery emerged. Interbreeding between white masters and African mistresses, then between whites and 'mulattos', produced a spectrum in which the brown-skinned descendant of, say, an Irish overseer was presumed to be socially superior to the black descendant of an African king. When the Caribbean islands gained independence after the Second World War, lighter-skinned people remained socially dominant.

4.10 The British (many Scots, Welsh and Irishmen were involved) brought with them the complex cultural situation of their own islands. British languages and dialects, British song and dance traditions, went into the creole fusion. But the earliest creole 'literature' clung to the emergent conventions of Standard English, as in the elegant historical and topographical writings of the planters Edward Long (a pioneer of 'scientific' racism) and Bryan Edwards in the eighteenth century. We know from examples given by such polished white writers that a vigorous creole 'folk poetry' already existed among the slave population. By the late nineteenth century, poetry in the vernacular was appearing in print, in local newspapers. The development of the 'West Indian tradition' since then can be summarized by reference to three moments:

(a) In 1931 a short-lived new Trinidadian journal *The Beacon* arose to encourage writing that would give authentic expression to West Indian life. In that decade, novels by C.L.R. James and Ralph de Boissière emerged from the *Beacon* movement.

(b) In 1942 Frank Collymore founded in Jamaica the first enduring literary journal of the Anglophone Caribbean, *Bim*. A.J. Seymour's journal *Kyk-over-al* followed in Guyana in 1945. There began to emerge a corpus of Caribbean verse by young talents rejecting the mentality and status of 'colonial subjects'.

(c) Meanwhile, from 1938 a Jamaican, Louise Bennett ('Miss Lou'), had practised as a newspaper-poet and public performer in the vernacular. Her forthright, witty use of creole was an inspiration for younger writers. (One of her poems, 'Back to Africa', is in the Poetry Anthology.) By 1967, when Edward Kamau Brathwaite published his book *Rights of Passage*, a bridge between 'oral' and 'literary' traditions could be made. The use of creole – 'nation language', as Brathwaite calls it – in public performance by 'serious' poets became important. It is associated with affirmation of African 'roots'. (You can see archive film of both Louise Bennett and Edward Kamau Brathwaite in TV11.)

4.11 Brathwaite adapted to popular culture, and other Caribbean poets have followed him in this path. Derek Walcott is one of those who have held back, insisting on the importance of European, as well as African, cultures and on a different role for the poet. This does not mean that Walcott is hostile to the vernacular (which he has used in many of his important plays) or to popular culture *per se*. It does mean that he has struggled in recent years to assert a special, personal position amid the immensely diverse vitality of Caribbean language usage. He recognizes the whole continuum as available for a poet's purposes, but will not commit himself to 'creole' or 'nation language' as his prime vehicle, or to the politicized medium of 'performance poetry'. In part his position relates to his very special origins. He was born and grew up on a 'British' island where the creole is French – 'patwa', *patois*.

Derek Walcott and *Another Life*

4.12   St Lucia (pronounced Saint Loo-sha) is one of the Windward Islands in the Lesser Antilles. It is only 27 miles by 14. Basically, it is a mass of partly submerged volcanic mountains, of which the highest is over 3000 feet. Carib resistance forced the first English settlers, in 1605, to abandon the island. A second attempt in 1638 was equally disastrous. The French were more successful in 1650, but the island changed hands incessantly between French and British in the colonial wars of the next century and a half (six times between 1782 and 1803 alone). In 1814 it came finally into British hands. But by this time the language of the island was a French-based creole, and the islanders were preponderantly Roman Catholic.

4.13   Derek Walcott was born in Castries, the island's small capital, in 1930, along with a twin-brother, Roderick. Their father, who died in the following year, was a member of the administrative middle class – a clerk of the First District Court. Their mother was headteacher of the infant school run by the small Methodist minority. Their descent – an important point for Walcott – was thoroughly mixed. A paternal grandfather was an Englishman from Barbados, a maternal grandfather was Dutch, from the very small island of Saint Maarten. The women in the family tree, however, were of predominantly African origin.

4.14   Walcott grew up well aware of the history of slavery, exploitation and cruelty that had created the culture of his native land. But his own experience of childhood as a British colonial was, he says, 'benign'. He has recalled how the unarmed native policeman in Castries represented the 'English bobby in the tropics' – polite, gentle, disciplined (*South Bank Show*). There was no sense for him of alienation from white culture. On the contrary: his father, an amateur painter, had collected reproductions of European pictures, and his mother was a great reciter and amateur actress fond of speaking Shakespeare. His own artistic ambitions developed very early, and were encouraged by his teacher. When he was eighteen he asked his mother for two hundred dollars so that he could publish a book of poetry. She somehow found them. It was printed in Trinidad. By the time he became a student at the University of the West Indies, Jamaica, he was already a known writer. His first play was published in 1951.

4.15   These biographical data are relevant to understanding his long poem, *Another Life*, published as a separate volume with twenty-three chapters in 1973. He had been writing it since 1965. It is the work of a man in (early) middle age looking back to a (largely) idyllic childhood and youth during which he dedicated himself to both poetry and painting, discarding the latter in favour of words. Walcott grew up with every reason to suppose that he was an exceptional person. His class, religion and the English language spoken in his family circle differentiated him sharply from other islanders. He was amply encouraged to believe that he was extremely talented, and he fully justified the faith of his mentors. He had good reason to compare himself to the great English Romantic poet Wordsworth who, at similar age, in his mid-thirties, had written in *The Prelude* an account of the 'growth of a poet's mind'.

4.16   But, as with Wordsworth, doubt and disillusion set in. Walcott experienced the political and creative frustrations of a Third World intellectual. Plans for a federation of the newly independent British West Indian islands broke down in the 1960s. Through processes brilliantly presented by V.S. Naipaul, from Trinidad, in his novel *The Mimic Men* (1967), the flaring hopes of small nations with new flags were dampened as local politicians struggled helplessly, or merely succumbed, in the face of pressure and manipulation from international capitalism. Walcott himself had a difficult, though creative, time as director of Trinidad Theatre Workshop (1959–77). The first three 'books' of *Another Life* present, largely in lyrical terms, a surge of young life towards success: in the last book, 'sadder and wiser' speakers confront despair and tragedy. Hence the title on one level refers us to a fissure in the poet's 'real' experience.

4.17   The life of his early days was also 'another life' distinct from the present. But I think the title has a further connotation. The life is 'other' to Walcott's because it is *fictionalized*. It is the autobiography of a poet who is not simply 'Walcott'. His fellow townsfolk and friends are given imaginary names. His twin-brother (also a playwright) is left out altogether. Experience, in short, has been ordered, rearranged, idealized and dramatized.

4.18   Yet the poem insists on being read as a highly personal statement – in this it is characteristic of all Walcott's non-dramatic verse. Its 'confessional' character links it, in the first place, with Wordsworth; secondly, with a tendency in more recent US verse. Walcott must have been aware, for instance, of Robert Lowell's astonishing *Life Studies* (1959) in which a major US poet confronted his own madness and its roots in childhood experience.

4.19   *Another Life* insists on a still wider range of reference and comparison. Of the epigraphs of its four books, only the last – a quotation from Matthew Arnold – refers us to a writer in English. The first is from a French novelist and aesthetician, André Malraux, the second and third are from major twentieth-century writers from Latin America – the novelist Alejo Carpentier, from Cuba, and the Peruvian poet Cesar Vallejo. Add references to Pasternak and to other Russian literature in the poem itself, and it is clear that Walcott aims to transcend the limitations of English-language culture. The tradition he calls on is international in scope. *Another Life* might be partly compared, in miniature, to the *Canto General* ('General song') of the Chilean poet Neruda (1950), which traverses the whole history of Latin America and presents the consciousness of a continent's people; in just such a way, Walcott gives voice or embodiment to St Lucia's extinct Caribs, dead redcoats, salty fishermen. He moves between the intensely personal and the cosmic.

4.20   Before you read our first excerpt, Chapter 7 (from Book One, 'The Divided Child'), you should know what has preceded it. In the first chapter we have met the narrator as a teenager, an aspirant painter, and have been present at the moment when his mentor Harry reads to him from a new book, *First Poems: Campbell* – the work of a Jamaican published on his home island in 1945, an important precedent in the development of West Indian literature:

> And from a new book,
> bound in sea-green linen, whose lines
> matched the exhilaration which their reader,
> rowing the air around him now, conveys,
> *another life it seemed would start again.*
>
> (*Another Life*, Chapter 1; my italics)

4.21   The second chapter movingly presents the narrator's mother. The third is an 'alphabet' of Castries characters, compared, in only half-jocular fashion, with the personages of Homer's epics: the imagination of the narrator makes 'the town's one clear-complexioned whore' into Helen of Troy, a 'tattooed ex-merchant sailor' into Odysseus. The fourth chapter deals with religion: the austere faith of the 'plain chapel' of the Methodists is set against the vivid images of Renaissance painters in Catholic Italy, and against the African magic, obeah – to which is attributed the death of Castries' richest merchant. Chapter 5 presents further vignettes of Castries life, then takes us on a coastal vessel making routine calls at the island's seaboard villages. Chapter 6 draws back to meditate on island life as a whole – sea and volcanoes, poverty and disease.

4.22   It's also helpful to know that 'Gregorias' is the narrator's close friend, a painter from his own generation (modelled on Walcott's own friend, the remarkable artist Dunstan St Omer), and that 'the crossing of that pair' in Section v of Chapter 7 refers to Dante's meeting with his ideal love Beatrice – a grand precedent for the narrator's meeting with the girl, 'Anna', evoked in the fourth. Chapter 7 shows us a 'divided child' growing up among venerated tokens of European and Christian religion, but yearning for 'African' roots.

ACTIVITY

Please now read Chapter 7 of *Another Life* (in the Poetry Anthology). As you do so, consider the following aspects of it:

(a)   The use of pronouns applied to the narrator. What is the effect of alternating between 'I' and 'he'? (You might concentrate on the first paragraph and on Section iv.)

(b)   Walcott's metres. What is the effect, do you think, of the striking metrical variations – as between, for instance, the first paragraph and Section iii?

DISCUSSION

Both factors create *instability* in the text. The steady affirmations of 'I' give way to descriptions of the adolescent dreams of 'he'. The 'he' undermines the authority of 'I'.

In Sections i and ii that basic English measure, the iambic pentameter, is always in our minds, much though Walcott varies from the standard ten-syllable iambic line with which both begin. Sections iii and iv are in 'free verse' without any regular pattern. Section v, by contrast, is patterned in a way that suggests an elaborate regular form that it doesn't in fact follow. The first four lines – rhymed *abba* so that short lines rhyme with long – remind me of certain deliberately strange effects in the verse of Thomas Hardy, and are very likely intended to, since Hardy is the pre-eminent poet in English of the pathos of youthful love remembered with hindsight. But there is no regularity thereafter (*cdefgded*), and in the last five lines (*hiihi*) Walcott takes the risk of using what is, in effect, the same rhyming syllable in both masculine ('heard') and feminine ('outward') instances. ('Masculine' signifies a rhyme between two syllables that would normally be stressed, for example 'below' and 'grow'. If, however, you rhyme 'portfolio' with 'grow', that is feminine rhyme. Yes, the terms *are* sexist.)

4.23   All this bears on the subject-matter of the chapter and the narrator's complex attitude towards it. We are to understand that the emotions evoked – a yearning for heroic suffering, a moment of self-transcendence amid 'Nature', a passion for Italian Renaissance painting, and 'first love' for a beautiful blonde girl – were truly intense, and important in the poet-narrator's development. Yet they are also viewed ironically, as the outcomes of limitation and ignorance. They are products of 'provincialism', a colonial situation, and also of adolescent eagerness and naïvety.

4.24 In Section i the ringing *authority* of the first line comes from 'English tradition', a tradition evoked by a pentameter such as the British Romantic poet Byron might have penned. St Lucia typifies the provinces that are peripheral to this tradition. Those within the tradition know what is 'real', what 'pseudo' epic. The first voice, 'I', of this chapter asks fellow inhabitants of the tradition for 'pardon'. ('He' was just a little colonial kid – he'd never *seen* a *real* autumn such as you get in Southern England: the third person pronoun distances the authority of the present from the silliness of the past.)

4.25 Yet in the second and third paragraphs, 'I' moves into complicity, surely, with the child who supposes the imagery of Romantic poetry to be as sacred as the True Cross is for Catholics? We are not to imagine a stuffed bird being actually held before a class by a teacher: the images of provincial museum and Mass are symbolic. The associations of the first – mournful and fusty – give way to the richer connotations of the second.

4.26 Fired by romanticism, the boy 'I' imagines himself as an imperial hero – an 'explorer' like Livingstone, threatened by savages. 'That life' for which he yearns to suffer is the one associated with the *imperialist* 'Word'. Yet, ironically, a Romantic quest for 'roots', for the 'natural man' and 'ancestral, tribal country', leads Walcott to identify, not with Cumberland peasants (as in Wordsworth's poetry) or Greek freedom fighters (as in Byron's) but with black people of African descent. The second section will mean a lot more if you've read Wordsworth's *The Prelude* and can remember the famous 'spots of time' in that very long poem – passages where the English poet recalls visionary moments in his youth. 'About the August of my fourteenth year' matches *exactly* – in metre, in matter-of-fact tone – the manner with which Wordsworth begins such recollections. I cannot identify the source of the quotation that begins 'darker grows the valley', but its deliberate intrusion heightens the sense that this is a very 'literary' passage. And yet, surely, it moves us and seems to reproduce, as well as to create, truly strong emotions? What it says is crucial to the whole of *Another Life*: the visionary poet is fastened inexorably to his people, to the poor. 'The taste of water is still shared everywhere' is a line of breathtaking power. We are all water-drinkers, all human 'for all that'.

4.27 Even so the vision dissolves into questioning. Samuel Palmer (again, I cannot place the quotation) was an English Romantic painter revered in the mid-twentieth century by English people for his depiction of a quintessentially Southern English landscape. If *that* is the 'true light', then the fantasies of a boy among St Lucian clouds are suspect, or worthless. The 'cold iron' of colonial reality enters the boy's soul. Twilight is 'bugle-coloured' because imperial garrisons sounded the last post. In this small island outpost, when empire went at last, it was not grandly: only clerks departed. Yet even these – with the Roman arches of colonial official architecture – represented an aesthetic domain for which the boy yearned, associating *their* twilight with famous paintings by Claude and Turner.

4.28 The obsession with painting is developed in the third section. I think art history is deliberately muddled here. The High Renaissance paintings of Raphael are remote from the much earlier works from Siena where painters surrounded saints with gold-leaf. But the reference to Fra Angelico in Section iv is, I am sure, meant to be precise. Typically, Angelico painted holy figures in blue and white. The reference conjures up for 'Anna', the schoolgirl with whom the narrator falls in love, a beautiful, meek, innocent white face.

4.29 She is 'Anna', in this poem, partly because she overlaps, in Walcott's imagery, with Anna Karenina. Tolstoy's heroine has memorable dealings with trains and railway stations.

ACTIVITY

Do you think that Section v, composed of a single rhetorical sentence, is successful? Consider both the movement of the verse and its content.

DISCUSSION

My own feeling is that the effect is strained. This section concludes the first book of *Another Life*. Walcott is trying to make it weighty, but I am more conscious of elaborate technique than of strongly created emotional force. The introduction of railway imagery into the context of Walcott's diminutive island seems to me incongruous, even absurd. Whether or not you agree with me that the passage is unsuccessful, its 'Europeanized', almost 'abstract' handling of the personage of Anna will be relevant when we consider Walcott's treatment, in his verse, of women. It's odd, isn't it, that a schoolgirl should be identified with Beatrice and Anna Karenina? She is 'Muse' for an aspirant poet rather than genuine girl.

4.30   The second book (Chapters 8–12) is called 'Homage to Gregorias'. Dunstan St Omer, the original for 'Gregorias', produced, of all West Indian painters, perhaps the most widely known Caribbean image – his altarpiece for the Roseau Valley Church in St Lucia, where the Mother of God is seen among black locals. Long before this (as Chapters 8, 9 and 10 of *Another Life* evoke), he and the young Walcott, drunk with both liquor and excitement, had committed themselves to expressing in art St Lucian landscape and life. The narrator records his own sense of failure, his recognition of Gregorias's superior talent.

ACTIVITY

We've seen that the retrieval of history is an important theme in new writings in English. Chapter 11 of *Another Life* expresses the narrator's complex youthful relationship with history. Please read it now. Walcott refers in Sections iii and iv to a specific and remarkable episode in Caribbean history. It occurred in 1651, not on St Lucia but on another small island, Grenada. The native Caribs had been tricked into selling the island to a French company. They rose against the white settlers and were massacred. Their band at last took refuge on a promontory, where about 40 – after a desperate last stand – jumped into the sea rather than submit. The place was thus known as Le Morne Des Sauteurs ('The hill of the jumpers'). Its name echoes that of the Morne over the harbour in Castries, a hill on which imperial garrisons had quartered, including the Fifth Regiment of Foot (the Northumberland Fusiliers) who had fought the French on the island in the 1770s, taking the white feathers, on one occasion, from the hats of their slain foes (see Section iii). 'Peccavi', incidentally (in Section v), is the Latin for 'I have sinned', the basis of a famous Imperial pun when Sir Charles Napier sent this one word to the authorities as his message after conquering Sind, in India, in 1843. Bryan Edwards, mentioned in Section i, was a white creole historian of the eighteenth century.

How, in this chapter, does the narrator's identification with the Caribs relate to his youthful 'nostalgia' for the heyday of the British Empire? Focus on the language of Section i, comparing it with that of Sections iv and v.

DISCUSSION

In Section i the play of adjectives, from 'irritable' onwards, suggests amusement, irony. In Section iv, the language is lyrical, rapt. The Caribs' behaviour is *like* that attributed to gallant redcoats only inasmuch as all examples of courage have a common factor – courage. The juxtaposition of the 'heroes' of imperialism with its victims is evidently ironic. But the requiem for the redcoats in Section v is clearly meant to be taken seriously.

I don't propose to go through all of Chapter 11 in detail. Sections i and ii evoke a schoolboy's identification with redcoat soldiers. Section iii puts distance between schoolboy and adult narrator, who can recognize 'ennui, defence, disease' in the lot of the common soldiers – who, in every campaign in the Caribbean, died far more often from disease than from bullets. But then comes the extraordinary Section iv.

So far, we've had leisurely free verse with an inclination towards iambic blank verse (for example, the iambic pentameters of 'a lonely Englishman who loved parades … When the war came the mouths began to bleed'). In Section iv rhythm is transformed along with point of view. The long lines (and the shift to 'we' in mid-section) recall the choruses of Greek tragedy. The reference to Thermopylae sets the fate of the Caribs (utterly defeated) alongside that of Leonidas' Spartans in Ancient Greece – who died, but stalled the Persian invaders and made ultimate victory possible. Before the battle, the Spartans were seen calmly combing their hair. This gesture is transferred to the Carib wind-god Hourucan, from whose name (as early as the mid-sixteenth century) our word 'hurricane' derived.

The headlong rush of this section represents, it seems, both exhilaration and confusion. The 'I' is initially that of a Carib who has created Gods from the earth and now – in disgust? in resignation? – destroys them. His heels have 'never hurt horses' since Caribs had none. The horses of the conquerors grind the Caribs into the earth as the Carib spokesman has ground their gods. When we arrive at:

> who am I, under
> such thunder, dear gods, under the heels of the thousand

The speaker seems to be no longer Carib, but an individual overpowered by history, sucked into movement beyond his control. The implication seems to be that 'this race' – the human race – embraces both Spartan and Carib, that history is marked by recurrent suicidal defiance, which is noble and necessary.

'I' becomes 'the child' in the last section, distanced again. Perhaps we can understand this chapter best by remembering a line from Chapter 7: 'What else was he but a divided child?' The child descends from both the victors (the British imperialists, now departed) and the defeated. The blood that rises in his beloved Anna's cheek is that of dead white soldiers. The narrator pronounces 'Peace' to the redcoats, will not arraign European imperialism.

4.31 Walcott's view of 'history' is defiantly unorthodox. He opposes its normal use by scholars, black and white. In an essay published in 1974, he seems to reject 'the idea of history as time for its original concept as myth … fiction, subject to a fitful muse, memory', and adds:

> I accept this archipelago of the Americas. I say to the ancestor who sold me and to the ancestor who bought me I have no father, I want no such father, although I can understand you black ghost, white ghost, when you both whisper 'history', for if I attempt to forgive you both I am falling into your idea of history which justifies and explains and expiates.
> (quoted in Baugh, 1978b, p.77)

I find Walcott's remarks on history, in this essay and elsewhere, very hard to understand. But the *emotional* force of his rejection of history as usually conceived seems to derive from impatience with fellow intellectuals obsessed with tracing African roots in Caribbean culture and repeatedly denouncing the horrors of the slave-trade and plantation life. For Walcott the New World is still a *new* world, an arena for celebrating the existing life rather than for harping on past misery. His narrator in *Another Life* and his friend Gregorias encounter St Lucia's landscape like two Adams in Eden, 'naming', giving definition to, natural phenomena as if for the first time. Art, not history, creates meaning.

4.32   Let's now move to Chapter 20, though before you read it you may like to look at the next few paragraphs for background. Intervening chapters have dealt with Walcott's *annus mirabilis*, his 'golden year' of 1948 when he left school, was in love with Anna and published his first book – the year also when four-fifths of Castries burnt to the ground, so that its former life became 'another life' as modern concrete buildings replaced what Walcott has called its 'ancient lyrical architecture'. By Book Four (Chapters 18–23) Walcott's narrator resides permanently away from the island. The book's title, 'The Estranging Sea', is taken from Matthew Arnold's 'To Marguerite':

> Who order'd that their longing's fire
> Should be, as soon as kindled, cool'd?
> Who renders vain their deep desire? –
> A God, a God their severance ruled!
> And bade betwixt their shores to be
> The unplumb'd, salt, estranging sea.

This famous Victorian poem projects the human individual as 'enisled' in the sea of life, cut off from union with his or her kind.

4.33   The first chapter of Book Four, Chapter 18, presents an imaginative picture of the last days of Harry Simmons, the one character in *Another Life* who goes by a 'real' name. Simmons (b.1914) was a St Lucian civil servant who was also part-time painter, botanist, butterfly-collector, folklorist, newspaper editor and antiquarian. He had helped Walcott and St Omer with their painting and had shown Walcott Campbell's book of poems, mentioned earlier. Eventually he left his job and withdrew to a hill-village to paint. In Chapter 18 Walcott thinks of him there as the archetypal artist panicking before his own work:

> the done with its own horror of the undone
> that frays us all to pieces and breakdown,
> all of us, always, all ways, one after one.

The narrator relates this to his own condition in middle age, disillusioned with his fellow Caribbeans – 'the spawn of slaves … spitting on their own poets, /preferring their painters drunkards…'

4.34   Chapter 19 is a 'busin' – a sustained exercise in invective in a well-recognized Caribbean mode of 'abusing' opponents so as to convert them. The narrator denounces populist Caribbean intellectuals who 'chafe and nurture the scars of rusted chains /like primates favouring scabs', who 'explain to the peasant why he is African … whose God is history':

> their vision blurs, their future is clouded with cataract,
> but out of its mist, one man,
> whom they will not recognise, emerges,
> and staggers towards his lineaments.

Who is this? It could be Simmons, achieving clear 'lineaments' in death. It could be the narrator/Walcott himself, 'staggering' towards identity. But we are likely to suppose that it is Gregorias, who 'staggers' into the next chapter. In any case, a (frankly, rather trite) conception of the misunderstood individual genius ahead of his time underlies the rhetoric. Walcott, like other 'new writers', is obviously interested in expressing the search for an identity; he is not alone among them in taking a Messianic view of the role of the 'Artist' who in his work expresses his people's identity and redeems it.

4.35 Walcott had been working on *Another Life* for a year when news came (not by letter, as in the poem, but in a phone call from his twin-brother Roderick) that Simmons had killed himself. At once Walcott realized that this death gave his poem shape: it became the keystone of the whole structure.

ACTIVITY

Read Chapter 20 of *Another Life* now. As you do so, make brief notes on (a) how the focus alters through the chapter, and (b) the literary, artistic and musical references: how would you describe their effect?

DISCUSSION

Chapter 20 is very obviously crafted. It moves from a situation where the poet is trapped in solipsism, in conceiving the world purely in relation to himself, to an elegy where he has wholly escaped from self-absorption and imagines Simmons as the spirit of his native island and all its people. Its literary references are grand, and deliberately obtrusive. A quotation from Hardy's 'During Wind and Rain' (which you met in Block 1) heads the chapter, and the thirteenth line begins with a phrase from the same poem. V.S. Naipaul is quoted. Reference is made to Boris Pasternak's autobiographical *Safe Conduct*, in which the Russian writer remembered the great revolutionary poet Mayakovsky, who had committed suicide. 'Fiery particle' echoes a phrase that Byron, reacting to the early death of Keats, uses to refer to the poet's soul. We are working up to an elegy in the grand manner, with Simmons elevated implicitly to Parnassus with Keats and Mayakovsky.

First, though, we have the live painter, Gregorias, visiting the narrator in Trinidad after years apart. The narrator's discomfort dominates this section. His affirmation of faith in Gregorias – 'They shine, they shine, /such men … honour the humbly great' – is almost choked by obscure cogitations and odd syntax. Walcott's syntax is often odd, loose, even ungrammatical. Here, the sentence beginning 'I write of a man…' is grammatical only if the subject of 'honour' is taken to be 'I', from which it is separated by six lines: the narrator 'honours' the 'humbly great' so as to 'venerate the good' and to 'render' (depict, reproduce) the 'simple flame' of virtue in an 'irresponsible citizen'. The awkwardness of all this suggests that the sentiment of 'I wished him dead … raged for his death' is still predominant, and with it the narrator's own self-hatred – he, more than Gregorias, may have betrayed in life and work the idealism of their shared youthful vision. The second section powerfully presents the narrator's personal despair through the imagery of bad weather. The third moves tentatively in thought towards the dead Harry.

At last, the narrator unleashes his grand elegy, with all the traditional authority of the blank verse iambic pentameter – seven of them, in fact, before the rhythm relaxes towards free verse. The reference to an illustrated medieval Book of Hours places Harry's death in a majestic (European) expanse of time and human reflection upon time. Looking at such a book in youth (Chapter 9) it had seemed part of 'another life', that of European art, brighter than St Lucia's; now its image of death as Reaper has come home to St Lucia.

The evocation and praise of Simmons that follow (in Section iv) release the man from the narrator's personal, possessive memory – 'Never to set eyes on this page, /ah Harry' – nobly into the life of his people.

Simmons the antiquarian is praised for returning objects to their 'tribal names' – presumably, to African ones. The reference to the fisherman 'with nothing between him and Dahomey...' suggests St Lucia's immediate relationship with Africa. Perhaps we are to understand that Simmons's closeness to the people (who 'had built him themselves') was genuinely symbiotic, unlike that of academic missionaries with tape-recorders. In any case, the finely phrased praise of Simmons conveys grief and admiration together in a way that makes emotional 'sense'.

Did you notice that word 'lacertilian? Perhaps because 'jut to his underlip' conveys in itself a strong picture, I must have read this passage at least a dozen times before I bothered to look up 'lacertilian' in the *OED*. It means 'appertaining to lizards, lizard-like'. I find that being sure of this reduces rather than increases the word's force. Its perky sound, evoking a combative yet subtle character, conveyed a *more* precise 'picture' than I can get from the dictionary definition – knowing which, I struggle to think how a man's mouth might be like a lizard's.

Mouths are important in this passage. The 'tongue' of the mandolin (a European instrument) is flavoured with white rum (typically Caribbean). This suggests a European voice touched with Caribbean tones. The 'young bay, parting its mouth' is 'young' because this is a *new* world, awaiting 'names' as infants do. The idea of the artist (or poet) as Adam, naming and ordering Creation, creating identities, is central to *Another Life*.

4.36   But large questions are begged here. Simmons 'returned' tribal names – originally given elsewhere – to common implements. Meanwhile, Simmons's people – the carpenter, the charcoal burner, the fisherman – use, as the narrator delicately admits ('*pour* Msieu'), a French *patwa*. In what sense can a folklorist like Simmons or poet like Walcott, using English, be seen as Adamic on behalf of these people? There is a problem here regarding Poet's relationship with People which cannot be resolved by setting up Simmons as an ideal.

4.37   It is not resolved in the last three chapters, where the narrator broods over the squalor and reek of St Lucia, over the loss of his first love Anna/ Andreuille (who became a nurse and never married), over the poet's vocation and over history. In the last chapter, returned as a 'prodigal' to St Lucia, the narrator, as much Walcott himself as he will ever be, addresses Walcott's friend St Omer, explains that he called him 'Gregorias' partly because it suggested 'a black Greek' (*ancient* Greek, that is) and reaffirms Messianically the validity of their shared youthful vision:

> Gregorias listen, lit,
> We were the light of the world!
> We were blest with a virginal, unpainted world
> With Adam's task of giving things their names ...

4.38   A strange idea that, 'naming' through painting. But by analogy it permits solution to the problem just mentioned: while Walcott cannot literally claim to have been Adam in 'naming' the island's places, produce and artefacts, his function has been Adamic in *describing*, 'painting', the landscape accurately and powerfully for the first time within 'literary tradition'. In other poems, he has acknowledged the richness of naming found in St Lucian *patwa*; he did this in 'Names', for example:

Listen, my children, say:
moubain: the hogplum,
cerise: the wild cherry,
baie-la: the bay,
with the fresh green voices
they were once themselves
in the way the wind bends
our natural inflections ...

(Walcott, *Sea Grapes*, 1976)

This poem, significantly, he dedicated to Edward Kamau Brathwaite who, you may recall, promotes Caribbean 'nation-languages', creoles. But, heads I win, tails you lose: there is a natural exuberance in the landscape which is not expressed by the names as such. The Adamic poet's role seems to be to go behind names already given to find the fresh greenness of a New 'New World'.

'The Schooner *Flight*'

ACTIVITY

'The Schooner *Flight*', from *The Star-Apple Kingdom* (1980), is one of Walcott's most important poems, perhaps his masterpiece. We looked briefly at part of it at the beginning of this section of Block 6; please now read all of it. (Note: a 'red nigger' is in the Caribbean someone of visibly mixed European and African descent.)

DISCUSSION

You may find it helpful to consider the following comments by another major poet, and contemporary of Walcott. Here is Seamus Heaney, reviewing *Star-Apple Kingdom*:

'The Schooner *Flight*', the long poem at the start of the book, is epoch-making ... I imagine he has done for the Caribbean what Synge did for Ireland, found a language woven out of dialect and literature, neither folksy nor condescending, a singular idiom evolved out of one man's inherited divisions and obsessions, an idiom that allows an older life to exult in itself and yet at the same time keeps the cool of 'the new' ...

For those awakening to the nightmare of history, revenge – Walcott has conceded – can be a kind of vision, yet he himself is not vengeful. Nor is he simply a patient singer of the tears of things. His intelligence is fierce but it is literary. He assumes that art is a power and to be visited by it is to be endangered, but he also knows that works of art endanger nobody else, that they are benign. From the beginning he has never simplified or sold short. Africa and England are in him. The humanist voices of his education and the voices from his home ground keep insisting on their full claims, pulling him in two different directions. He always had the capacity to write with the elegance of a Larkin and make himself a ventriloquist's doll to the English tradition which he inherited, though that of course would have been an attenuation of his gifts, for he also has the capacity to write with the murky voluptuousness of a Neruda and make himself a romantic tongue, indigenous and awash in the prophetic. He did neither, but made a theme of the choice and the impossibility of choosing. And now he has embodied the theme in the person of Shabine, the poor mulatto sailor of the *Flight*, a kind of democratic West Indian Ulysses, his mind full of wind and poetry and women. Indeed, when Walcott lets the sea-breeze freshen in his imagination, the result is a poetry as spacious and heart-lifting as the sea-weather at the opening of Joyce's *Ulysses*, a poetry that comes from no easy evocation of mood but from stored sensations of the actual:

> In idle August, while the sea soft,
> and leaves of brown islands stick to the rim
> of this Caribbean, I blow out the light
> by the dreamless face of Maria Concepcion
> to ship as a seaman on the schooner *Flight* ...

It is a sign of Walcott's mastery that his fidelity to West Indian speech now leads him not away from but right into the genius of English. When he wrote these opening lines, how conscious was he of another morning departure, another allegorical early-riser? The murmur of Malvern is under that writing, for surely it returns to an origin in *Piers Plowman*:

> In summer season, when soft was the sun,
> I rigged myself up in a long robe, rough like a sheep's,
> With skirts hanging like a hermit's, unholy of works,
> Went wide in this world, wonders to hear.
> But on a May morning, on Malvern Hills,
> A marvel befell me – magic it seemed.
> I was weary of wandering and went for a rest
> Under a broad bank, by a brook's side;
> And as I lay lolling, looking at the water,
> I slid into a sleep ...
>
> (Heaney, 1989, pp.23–5)

Heaney (a 'wood-kerne /escaped from the massacre' in Ulster) and Walcott (from one of the world's smallest independent countries) have both taught in rich North East American universities. They know and admire each other personally. It is no slur on their integrity to point out that the arena in which they meet and address verses to each other is somewhat rarefied. Yet Heaney sees 'dialect' as integral to Walcott's writing – 'I imagine he has done for the Caribbean what Synge did for Ireland...' He sees clearly how varied Walcott's application of the language is. And he spots a crucial echo at the start of the poem. When Walcott goes back to the medieval alliterative allegory, *Piers Plowman* (which Heaney, strangely, quotes in a modern translation), he refers to the linguistic uncertainty of the fourteenth century from which, as we have seen, David Dabydeen found inspiration to write in creole. Edward Kamau Brathwaite's rather barbed aside on this is worth noting: in a talk given at Harvard in 1979, he said that Langland had 'recently inspired Derek Walcott to his first nation-language effort' (Brathwaite, 1984, pp.9–10). Brathwaite sees Chaucer's pentameter as inimical to Caribbean self-expression: reverting to Langland, Walcott can be said to clear the way for the creole, 'nation-language' voice.

You will be returning to Heaney himself in Block 8. At that stage you might think about how his predicament relates to Walcott's 'impossibility of choosing'. In the latter's work Heaney respects and supports, as his review goes on to show (p.28), the tendency to turn away from 'inchoate communal plight' to 'refine the rhetoric' that is a poet's major tool. And yet Heaney relishes the 'democratic' voice given to Shabine.

4.39 The tensions we've been looking at are powerfully present in 'The Schooner *Flight*' – between 'art' and 'life', English and the vernacular. There is another aspect of the poem that demands argument – Walcott's, or Walcott/Shabine's, attitude towards women. Where do they fit into the great project of elevating a whole nation by fulfilling oneself as a poet?

4.40 Stewart Brown (1988/9, pp.10–15) has made a most interesting defence of Walcott against critics – mostly Caribbean – who have accused him of élitism and arrogant individualism, of 'being unable because of his class, colour and philosophy to "ground" with the West Indian people'. Brown sees Walcott as committed to the role of '*true* patriot', one who stands out for particular ideas and values that he believes serve the best interests of his community, no matter how unfashionable or outrageous they may seem. He notes three distinct 'inflections of voice' in Walcott's works which express this patriotism:

(a) *The Simple Patriot*: 'essentially the voices ... that assert Walcott's commitment to the Caribbean as his home and try to contribute to the creation of values that might shape the emerging independent societies'.

(b) *The Spoiler*: a people's patriot, 'withering into truth' those he sees as corrupting the possibilities for real development that exist/ed in the Caribbean.

(c) *The Fortunate Traveller*: the exiled patriot who tries to speak for the Caribbean – even the whole Third World – in the courts of the powerful.

It's the second 'inflection' that is relevant to 'The Schooner *Flight*'. 'Spoiler' was a dead Trinidadian calypso singer whose voice Walcott resurrected in 'The Spoiler's Return', a caustic satire on the post-independence Caribbean published in his book *The Fortunate Traveller* (1981). Brown traces the 'Spoiler' voice in some of Walcott's earlier poetry. He finds it in Chapter 19 of *Another Life*.

4.41 The 'Spoiler' voice is implicitly addressed to a *West Indian* readership, which alone can respond to its allusions and the nuances of its invective, its 'busin' and its 'picong' (from the French *piquant*). Shabine's voice in the first three sections of 'The Schooner *Flight*' is predominantly the 'Spoiler' voice.

4.42 Shabine is from Trinidad, from the island where the calypso has been a key form in popular culture. Walcott himself spent many years working there. On this island – though a little French patois has been spoken into the twentieth century – an English-related 'language continuum' exists. Walcott doesn't get into 'thick' creole. But his Shabine is unmistakably a user of creole grammatical forms:

> ... the cold sea rippling like galvanize ...
> I pass me dry neighbor sweeping she yard ...
> I taking a sea bath, I gone down the road ...

However, Shabine is also a poet. He tells us firmly at the end of the first section that he is writing this poem 'in common language', not of the people but 'the wind'. The movement anticipated in the first three sections is *from* a Trinidad in which both rich and poor are corrupt (a movie projector breaking down is more likely to provoke the poor to violence than the delinquencies of politicians) *to* a clean world of wind, salt and sea.

ACTIVITY

Walcott once wrote a poem called 'Homage to Edward Thomas'. When Shabine reaches Barbados in Section 6 and contemplates casuarina trees, Walcott ventriloquizes him into singing back to them in a way that recalls Thomas's 'Old Man', which you will remember from Block 3. The rhythms of the verse remind us of Thomas. The point made is different but related. What is it? (You will find it useful to go back to my discussion of Thomas's poem in Block 3.)

DISCUSSION

In 'Old Man', meditation on the plant leads Thomas to express a sense of the nameless, unnameable, dark core of human experience. Walcott in this section clarifies, I think, something implicit in the passages concerned with 'naming' in *Another Life*. *All* names are in a sense accidents, he says:

> ... to the wind
> whatever grief bent them was all the same,
> since they were trees with nothing else in mind ...

But when colonials gave names to local trees, it was painfully important for them to choose words with classical ('cypress') or biblical ('cedar') connotations. And though it is an 'inferior love' that values natural, growing things for such associations rather than for themselves, nevertheless this 'accident of naming' plays a crucial part in giving identity. Typically, slave-owners gave house-slaves such classical names as Scipio or Hannibal. (Both these heroes were African-born.) If black people behaved with the valour and dignity of such figures, they might 'by careful mimicry ... become men'.

We must not assume that Walcott is straightforwardly asserting the superiority of European classicism to native creole sensibility. He has said in an interview:

> As a young assistant master at St Mary's College [in St Lucia] teaching Latin to young black kids one felt that perhaps you're teaching them something not only that isn't natural to them but also that the last gasp or cry of a man dying would be in his natural language. You know you wouldn't die in Latin. You'd die in creole.
>
> (*The Guardian*, 9 July 1988)

Shabine, we may assume, is used to dramatize an argument that Walcott finds interesting and that relates to his preoccupation with naming. It is useful to think of the mature Yeats in this connection. In verse sequences, in his prime, Yeats powerfully expressed, sometimes through personae, contradictory positions – to none of which he was finally committed.

However, Section 7 of 'The Schooner *Flight*' clearly refers back to the 'Anna' episodes in *Another Life*, and there is no doubt that these are based on the young Walcott's actual relationship with a white girl, Andreuille, who became a nurse in Castries.

ACTIVITY

Please now read Elaine Savory Fido's 'Macho attitudes and Derek Walcott' in the Reader (pp.288–94). On the basis of what you've now seen of Walcott's work, can you agree with her case that Walcott is 'macho'?

DISCUSSION

I think Fido's argument, very moderately and fairly made, is convincing. Maria Concepcion and other Trinidad women in 'The Schooner *Flight*' are seen only in terms of sexuality, delicious or threatening. The gesture in Section 7 is poetically elegant, not humanly very satisfactory. Is it just that Shabine/Walcott leaves to 'you whom I loved first' (Anna) his works? (And in what sense – physically, in book form?) Or is it that she *was* 'poetry', no more no less, 'muse' not reality – a necessary prompter of verse, like Dante's Beatrice or Shakespeare's Dark Lady?

Walcott is conscious, as *Another Life* shows, of his own tendency towards solipsism. In the final section of the poem, Shabine grandiloquently proclaims:

> ... I am satisfied
> if my hand gave voice to one people's grief.

He pours his blessing on all the islands, but insists 'I have only one theme'. This 'theme' appears to be the search for transcendence and peace. The mystical isolation with which the poem ends is how a resigned man, alone, might meet death. Transcendence would be such as Shelley, in 'Adonais', accorded to the dead Keats when he said 'he is made one with nature'.

I do not think that Walcott goes all the way with this. The convenience for him of the Shabine persona seems to be that the proletarian poet can go further than his ventriloquist in expressing this Romantic conception of the poet, and be kept at a little distance. Even Shabine clears a space between himself 'satisfied' (with a socially useful role) and himself in Section 9 (mad, threatening all Trinidad with the absolute power of his poetry). These spaces permit an irony that enables the poem's risky project to work. We can enjoy the humorous and satirical low-life realism and the ultra-Walcottian lyricism without committing ourselves either to a fictionally 'realistic' Shabine or to a bardic view of poetry.

4.43   The *instability* of Walcott's poetry, which I remarked on when discussing Chapter 7 of *Another Life*, seems to me a saving rather than a damaging quality. His *rhetorics* – plural – are usually powerful in themselves: contending with each other they correct each other's excesses. I can always find fresh cause for intellectual and ethical unease when I re-read 'The Schooner *Flight*', whether in the exploitation of a 'Spoiler' persona, in the treatment of women, or in its conception of 'poetry'. But its language, section by section, is brilliantly handled. I would set it beside major poems by Yeats which are similarly disturbing, equally eloquent. However, the 'Modernist' masters directly evoked in the poem are Blok, a Russian poet associated with the 1917 revolution, and Eliot (Maria Concepcion's *Book of Dreams* contains the Tarot symbols referred to in *The Waste Land*). Shabine, associating himself with 'the drowned sailor' during the storm, is associated in turn by knowing readers with Eliot's Phlebas the Phoenician. Along with Walcott's 'Adamic' aspirations to freshness, newness, comes the ancient and modern poet's habit of allusion. Could any reader but a learned one grasp how echoes of Langland, Eliot and Edward Thomas contribute to the poem's effect? Walcott's self-conscious evocation of 'English tradition' does, in the last analysis, set him apart from many other Caribbean poets, of his own and younger generations. For these others, West Indian oral tradition and the spirit of 'Miss Lou' (Louise Bennett) are treated as jetties from which to launch.

4.44   In fairness, the last word may go to Walcott, in an essay published in 1972:

> Pastoralists of the African revival should know that what is needed is not new names for old things, or old names for old things, but the faith of using the old names anew, so that mongrel as I am, something prickles in me when I see the word Ashanti as with the word Warwickshire, both separately intimating my grandfathers' roots, both baptising this neither proud nor ashamed bastard, this hybrid, this West Indian. The power of the dew still shakes off our dialects ...
>
> (Walcott, 1972, p.10)

AUDIO-CASSETTE

You may find it useful to listen again to Audio-cassette 3 Side 2 on 'The Schooner *Flight*'.

Grace Nichols

4.45 We'll now discuss one of the West Indian poets who – without necessarily rejecting Walcott's verse wholesale – make very different assumptions about the role of the poet and his or her relationship to Caribbean people in general.

4.46 Grace Nichols was born in Guyana in 1950, one of seven children. She began to write as a journalist on a newspaper there, then worked for the government information services, where employees put out a small magazine. Here she published some poems and a short story. In 1977 she moved to the UK. Her first volume of poems, published by a small 'black press', Karnak House, won the Commonwealth Poetry Prize in 1983. Since then her verse has been published by the best known 'women's press', Virago.

4.47 To be *black* is to be disadvantaged in British society. A black *woman* is disadvantaged even within the black community. African mythologies and creation myths subordinate women as effectively as the Book of Genesis (Gilroy, 1989, p.15). Grace Nichols's first book, *I is a Long-memoried Woman*, is a sequence linking present-day women's consciousness in the Caribbean with the African past and the history of slavery. One publisher turned it down on the grounds that a male poet, Edward Kamau Brathwaite, had already covered this journey in *The Arrivants*, his trilogy! Nichols has pointed to the neglect of black women in literature and their exceptional problems in getting published:

> It's only within the last twenty years, since the women's movement, that in Europe you've had the upsurge of white women writers. You have presses like Virago, the Women's Press. In the Caribbean, where you don't have these kinds of facilities, black women have had less opportunity to be published.
>
> (Nichols, 1988, p.18)

Nevertheless, Nichols is aware of highly successful black American women writers – Alice Walker, Maya Angelou and Toni Morrison (whose novel you will read in Block 7).

ACTIVITY

Please now read in the Poetry Anthology 'Waterpot', 'Loveact', 'Skin-teeth', 'Sugar Cane' and 'Like a Flame'. These are five of the fifty-one poems in *I is a Long-memoried Woman*. They refer to the experience of women in the period of plantation slavery. Consider as you read:

(a)   How would you compare the language of the poems with Walcott's?

(b)   Do you see anything in the verse, as printed, to make you think that it was created with reading aloud in mind?

(c)   How would you describe the attitude towards men implicit in the poems?

DISCUSSION

(a)   The language, both in vocabulary and syntax, is much plainer, more direct, less 'poetic' than Walcott's. 'Creole' touches, however, are light and few.

(b)   In 'Loveact', two lines are punctuated by strokes to mark pauses. This might be seen as an alternative, adopted for the sake of neatness on the page, to Nichols's practice in 'Sugar Cane', where the division into short lines (in Section 4, one word-lines) gives very clear indication of the pace and emphasis of delivery required.

(c)   This is the most complex question. To consider it poem by poem:

(i)   In 'Waterpot', the woman's struggle is first of all with her circumstances, and with herself. In Africa, famously, women have such strong and erect carriage that they can carry waterpots on their heads without losing the liquid. The overseer, white and male, sneers at the assertion of dignity in her posture.

(ii)   African 'magic' – charms, poisons and rituals – was imported to the New World with the slaves, whose obeah doctors and voodoo priests seemed to white masters horribly sinister. Not without reason: slaves who were apparently docile nursed strong desires for revenge. But I think Nichols does not necessarily mean us to believe that the woman in 'Loveact' physically poisons the master and his family. In the 'human triangle', initially the 'mistress wife' is strongest, the master strong, the slave superficially weakest. But then her sensual attraction makes her 'the fuel /that keep them all going'. Now strongest, she can make life hard for them. The threat in 'Skin-teeth' is similar but more direct.

(iii)   However, 'Sugar Cane' and 'Like a Flame' debar us from assuming that Nichols is a prophet of a kind of female self-assertion that returns cruelty for cruelty. 'Sugar Cane' is an emblematic poem which subtly matches the life cycle of the plant with features of male psychology. It is commonly asserted (for instance, by the male Barbadian Brathwaite in his long sequence *Mother Poem*) that, in Caribbean society during and after slavery, it was the strength and compassion of women, rearing families with little or no help from overworked, absent or drunken fathers, that held things together. The cane represents a man outwardly hard, inwardly desperate (Section 1); his conditions of life are horrible (Section 2); despite *and* because of women's attentions, he is doomed (Section 3); yet (Section 4) he manages painfully to acquire self-knowledge; finally, he is released into sensual relationship with his mistress, the wind. That Nichols approves of such sensuality is beyond doubt. 'Like a Flame' directly presents the flash of sexual attraction felt by a woman for a male fellow worker in the canefields.

ACTIVITY

Please now read 'Grease' and 'Even Tho' from the Poetry Anthology (these are taken from Nichols's third volume of verse, *Lazy Thoughts of a Lazy Woman*, 1989). You see in these how such direct expression of sensuality is characteristic of her. 'Grease' is a wonderfully witty little poem, associating sensuality with laziness and stickiness – and ironically affirming these. Feminine virtue is not to be equated with a clean house. 'Even Tho' defines the limits of sensual abandon, insists on the woman's retention of independence *vis à vis* her lover – but does so in fruitily sensual terms.

Finally, look at the remaining examples of Nichols's work, which are from a sequence of seventeen, *The Fat Black Woman's Poems*, published in 1984. Nichols has said:

> I have my humorous side. It comes out in *A Fat Black Woman* for example and some people or critics can't seem to come to terms with it. People have said to me, *I is a Long-memoried Woman* is such a moving and deep book, and *A Fat Black Woman*, a few people have said, or told other poets, doesn't carry forward the struggle of black people …

> I hate the one-dimensional stereotype of the black woman as just being a sufferer or a person who's a victim or who's had a very oppressive history and she's carrying all these scars on her back, because I know that not to be

true – We black women have had to bear more than our fair share of burdens, but I know so many black women who are such rich humorous beings inside that I can't identify with that kind of stereotype image.

(1988, p.19)

More even than the *Long-memoried Woman* poems, those of *The Fat Black Woman* need to be imagined in performance. (You hear Nichols read in TV14.) Not that their jokes are unsubtle. When she goes shopping, the reference to her curses in 'Swahili/Yoruba and nation language ... all this journeying and journeying' genially makes fun of the 'back to Africa' elements in the poetry of Brathwaite and of Nichols herself: the 'journey' from one store to another is jestingly compared to the middle passage and the sea-voyages that brought West Indian immigrants to Britain. The word 'heritage' in 'Invitation' likewise implies light-heartedness about the grave matter of 'black identity'. But 'Tropical Death' asserts 'black identity' clearly enough. The sensuality that the fat black woman shares with other women in Nichols's books extends even beyond the grave: she wants a full-blooded Caribbean funeral, with night after night of 'bawl' and 'wake'.

4.48 You will later find it interesting to compare Nichols, as a witty woman poet effective in public performance, with Stevie Smith, whom you'll hear reading on Audio-cassette 4 Side 1. Smith has been marginalized in England as an 'eccentric', and her poetic tactics and strategies played on her position as rather a 'dotty female'. Nichols jests about her own 'fatness' and 'laziness', but not in such a way as to court or accept marginalization. I think there are two general (as distinct from personal, temperamental) reasons why she can radiate confidence and control. One is the women's movement, and the growth of women's publishing and an audience for women's poetry, since the 1960s. Witty women joking about men are part of a mainstream now, in no way eccentric. Secondly, Nichols, and other black Caribbean women poets, are part of a 'tradition', recently matured, in which a key figure has been a woman, Louise Bennett. It is a tradition imbued with 'orality', in which the ironic voice of 'Miss Lou' sets a precedent for relaxed, humorous confrontation with important issues. Nichols has said:

The Caribbean has such a rich oral heritage ... market scenes come out in poetry by Caribbean poets, and in novels, because it's very much a vibrant part of our culture. Even now I can hear the voices of the market women. We have all these [children's] rhymes and Caribbean talk and orality in our heads.

(Nichols, 1988, p.20)

As we have seen, she uses creole forms lightly, and creole vocabulary very little. But the rhythm of her reading, represented by line breaks on the page, is intended to evoke creole speech. She manifestly belongs on the same platform – literally – as male poets evoking 'orality', as diverse as Brathwaite, James Berry and Lynton Kwesi Johnson, and with women such as Jean Binta Breeze. Hers isn't a Messianic voice: it refers itself to common experience and common speech and offers entertainment as well as 'consciousness-raising'.

Conclusion

4.49 Throughout Section 4, you'll have been aware that the 'language issue' in Caribbean poetry is important. Walcott is a writer who seems, by comparison with English contemporaries such as Larkin and Hill, drastically different, even radical – in his affirmations of the value of poor people and in his readiness to use non-standard forms of English and to relate his own work to that of calypso singers. Yet in the West Indian context he has plausibly been attacked as a conservative. Your work on his poetry and on Nichols's should enable you to begin weighing the arguments. I leave you with my personal view. I agree with Joseph Brodsky that poetry is the 'essence of world culture' – the most 'universal' and necessary of cultural forms. But within world culture, I see the elaborate 'traditions' of printed poetry in the European languages as enticing but exceptional. As a fellow countryman of Robert Burns and Sorley MacLean, I concur with both of them that the basis of poetry is oral and popular. And I am not sure that Walcott – drawn to relate the St Lucians around him to the heroes and heroines of Homer whose *oeuvre* has come down out of ancient Greek oral tradition – would actually disagree. In 1990 he published a poem of 325 pages, *Omeros*, in which St Lucian fishermen with Greek names are assimilated with ancient epic. 'The taste of water is still shared everywhere.'

5   Caribbean voices II: 'In a Free State'

Approaching V.S. Naipaul

5.1   In September 1960 V.S. Naipaul returned to his home country, Trinidad, after ten years in England. He was on a visit funded by the Trinidad government. While he was there the premier, Dr Eric Williams, a historian, proposed that he write a non-fiction book about the Caribbean. Naipaul, at twenty-eight, was already widely known as an author, with two novels and a collection of short stories behind him. He had just completed what was to become a 'classic' and his most popular work, *A House for Mr Biswas* (1961). This was a richly humorous, semi-autobiographical account of the impact of change upon an enclosed, traditional East Indian family from rural Trinidad – Naipaul's own background. For all the enjoyment of its subject, however, and the brilliant accuracy of its account of this particular Caribbean subculture, *Biswas* revealed a level of irony and disillusion that might have warned its Caribbean audience, at least, of what was to come. But *The Middle Passage* (1962), Naipaul's 'impressions' of five colonial countries in the West Indies and South America, shocked and dismayed West Indians at home and abroad for its acid dismissal of Caribbean culture, history and society. Even more upsetting was the enthusiastic reception it received from English and US critics, who praised its critical detachment and descriptive power.

5.2   This highlights the main problem involved in approaching Naipaul's writing. He is unquestionably the best-known and most prolific Anglophone writer of the Caribbean, with about twenty books, innumerable articles and most of the major English literary awards (and a knighthood) behind him. Far from making him a cultural hero, however, the nature and impact of his work have made him among the most problematic, if not actually disliked, of Caribbean authors:

> I never liked Naipaul. I could never read him without a sense of self-
> betrayal, I could not enter into his stories without being turned off from
> myself ... I was just beginning to come out of the self-hate that colonialism
> had implanted in me when I first encountered Naipaul – a fellow colonial

who knew my condition better than I did, described it with a fine and acute understanding, and then delivered me up to my subjugation in the pursuit of his own deliverance.

(Sivanandan, 1990, p.33)

5.3   It is more than just a question of Naipaul's criticism of post-independence Caribbean society, of a Third World writer attacking his homeland. Chinua Achebe has become increasingly critical of post-independence Nigeria; so, too, has Wole Soyinka, whose *Madmen and Specialists* spares nobody in its attack upon his self-seeking, war-mongering compatriots. Yet their writings also express a powerful and intimate sense of belonging to specific, living cultures, as their use of traditional Igbo and Yoruba ritual, legend and myth suggests. And their voices are recognized, listened to, as such. Is it that the Caribbean writer has lost even these surviving, alternative traditions with which to oppose or transform the colonial inheritance? Transplanted, and enslaved or indentured, those brought in to replace the massacred original inhabitants of the West Indies have lost their customs and languages, their cultures, and so they cannot be expected to express more than the inevitable alienation and despair consequent on that loss – or so the argument might run. But as we have just seen from the writings of Derek Walcott and Grace Nichols, it is perfectly possible for Caribbean voices to establish, even celebrate, their own past and multitudinous traditions. And this is as true for writers based in the West Indies as it is for those who have gone abroad. How, then, to approach a Caribbean voice that sums up the history of the Caribbean thus: 'Nothing was created in the West Indies' (1969b, p.29)?

5.4   Criticism of Naipaul is apparent from the beginning of his career. Thirty years before Sivanandan, George Lamming observed in *The Pleasures of Exile*:

> His books can't move beyond castrated satire; and although satire may be a useful element in fiction, no important work … can rest safely on satire alone. When such a writer is a colonial, ashamed of his cultural background and striving like mad to prove himself through promotion to the peaks of a 'superior' culture whose values are gravely in doubt, then satire is for me nothing more than a refuge. And it is too small a refuge for a writer who wishes to be taken seriously.
>
> (Lamming, 1960, p.225)

'Superior' is in scare quotes to emphasize that this borrowed superiority comes from a culture whose values are 'gravely in doubt'. This is an 'end of empire' viewpoint, if you like; it is a 'post-colonial' perspective. And it continues to frame the predominant response to Naipaul's work, right up to the present, from those who perceive themselves to be outside the Anglo-American, metropolitan centres of power.

5.5   Our own responses will depend on our contexts: our own situation, history and ideology must inevitably come into play here. Arguably, this is always the case. But Naipaul's writings push us towards becoming more aware of this context, push us sharply and disturbingly. And *that*, I want to argue, is the most important reason why we should attend to his voice.

5.6   Lamming's remarks were made in response to Naipaul's first two novels, *The Mystic Masseur* (1957) and *The Suffrage of Elvira* (1958). Both works took a comic but jaundiced look at the workings of British-style democratic processes in the Caribbean – a view that coincided with nationalist fervour and rising expectations in the West Indies and among West Indians (such as Lamming) abroad. The focus of these first two novels was the rural Indian community, their aim to show up the squalid corruption and trickery of post-war politics in Trinidad, or Elvira as it is called. 'Democracy had come to Elvira four years before, in 1946', the narrator coolly observes; 'but it had taken nearly everybody by surprise and it wasn't until 1950, a few months before the second general election under universal adult franchise, that people began to see the possibilities' (*The Suffrage of Elvira*, 1969a, p.12). These 'possibilities' turn out to be the making of money and the pursuit of power.

5.7   When Naipaul returned to the Caribbean and wrote *The Middle Passage*, the interests and themes of his preceding fiction were picked up and sharpened, even to the extent of repeating some phrases:

> Nationalism was impossible in Trinidad. In the colonial society every man had to be for himself; every man had to grasp whatever dignity and power he was allowed; he owed no loyalty to the island and scarcely any to his group. To understand this is to understand the squalor of the politics that came to Trinidad in 1946 when, after no popular agitation, universal adult suffrage was declared. The privilege took the population by surprise. Old attitudes persisted ...
>
> (*The Middle Passage*, 1969b, p.78)

This generalizing, cynical and sarcastic note is what most offended those who, like Lamming, felt themselves part of the rising nationalist movement of the post-war period, and whose own writings contributed to it. It is as if Naipaul was stuck within what Fanon called the first phase of interaction between the metropolitan and colonial cultures – successfully assimilating European modes of expression, but not going on to assert an identity, much less becoming Fanon's revolutionary 'awakener of the people' (Reader, 'On national culture', p.271).

5.8   Things are not quite so simple, however. We've seen how Derek Walcott may be counted as a major voice from the Caribbean. We've also seen how one of the many accents of that voice is a satire where he fuses the learned, literary, high-cultural European tradition and the popular, oral forms of the Caribbean. One of the best examples of this is 'The Spoiler's Return' (1981), which Angus Calder mentioned as another version of Shabine's vehement, allusive, truth-telling voice in *Another Life*. In 'The Spoiler's Return', the persona of a famous Trinidadian calypso-singer from the forties and fifties, Theophilus Phillip or 'The Mighty Spoiler', is used for a witty exploration of how the Caribbean might appear if the Spoiler were to return. At first he finds that 'nothing ain't change but colour and attire'; and the old round of exploitation seems to be continuing as before. So, he muses:

> I see these islands and I feel to bawl,
> 'area of darkness' with V.S. Nightfall.

An Area of Darkness (1964) is the book Naipaul went on to write about his first visit to his grandfather's homeland, India, an 'area of darkness' to him as a child growing up in rural Trinidad and later the focus of his often bitter criticism. The phrase is adapted by Walcott here to suggest the dark and gloomy, not to say apocalyptic, pronouncements on Caribbean society and culture for which Naipaul soon became so well-known at home and abroad. But for Walcott (in the Spoiler's words), 'this ain't the Dark Age, is just Trinidad'.

5.9   In the end, Walcott celebrates his place, his complex inheritance. His satire is critical, subversive, but it allows for something positive too, for acceptance. Naipaul's voice is also often satiric, as Lamming says. But it does not accept; and towards the Caribbean it has an undeniably negative accent. This is why, even though Walcott acknowledges the critical force of this other major voice from the Caribbean, he distances himself from it. On the other hand, however much he may disagree with Naipaul's viewpoint, Walcott acknowledges its presence and the reasons why it is possible to take up such a position. Whatever Caribbean writers may think of Naipaul, his is a voice they cannot ignore. This is why, for example, the Caribbean critic Selwyn Cudjoe – who has no doubts about Naipaul's limitations, his prejudices, arrogance, reactionary politics, and so on – nevertheless insists:

> it is necessary to understand the forces that shape his work and the issues with which he is concerned – Like it or not, Naipaul's work represents an important post-colonial impulse/response that begs to be understood and interpreted.
>
> (Cudjoe, 1988, pp.xiii–xiv)

Indeed it does; and that is what I will be trying to do here.

5.10 According to Cudjoe, Naipaul's position (or 'major problematic') has remained the same: 'Who or what am I in this colonial world?' And yet, argues Cudjoe, the meaning of his work is never 'given', it must be 'progressively discovered' (p.5). The point is that Naipaul's specific Trinidadian origins have indelibly marked his work; but Trinidad has been overtaken by India, Africa, South America, Iran, Pakistan – and England and North America. This larger, international terrain is the *post-colonial* world, the terrain of the book we are going to study here – *In a Free State*.

ACTIVITY

But first, if you haven't read Edward Said's 'Yeats and decolonization', it would be helpful if you did so (Reader, pp.34–41). Said suggests that earlier writers such as Yeats and Fanon do not show how the new political order can achieve 'moral hegemony' after decolonization, which leaves us with at least 'part of the difficulty we live with today in Ireland, Asia, Africa, the Caribbean, Latin America and the Middle East'.

5.11 But *In a Free State*, ranging worldwide in its account of decolonization, does engage with the 'new order' of our times. 'Who or what am I in this *post-colonial* world?' That is its central concern. The result may not make anyone feel very cheerful – although *In a Free State* is not without a mordant, ironic humour. But it does provide a further perspective on the themes that interest us in this block – identity, history, cultural conflict and assimilation, exile, language. *In a Free State* is 'post-colonial' because the book takes as its starting-point the end of empire, and raises the question of what kind of freedom the departure of the colonizer has left, a question applied to the First World as well as the Third World, to the past as well as the present. What is Naipaul's answer to this? It isn't easy to say, even after you have read the book. Before you begin, there are the ambiguities of the title, in which 'state' may refer to a political entity or a psychological condition, or both. And this is only one of a series of puzzling ambiguities that confront the reader approaching *In a Free State* for the first time.

ACTIVITY

If you haven't already read *In a Free State*, please do so now. In what follows I will be expecting you to *re-read* sections, as we consider in more detail what to make of it.

A citizen of the world

5.12 First of all, let us consider what 'new voice' we have in this book. The moment you open the first few pages of *In a Free State*, it becomes clear that here is a kind of 'new writing', a 'voice' which is different from those you have so far come across in Block 6. This is particularly clear if you recall for a moment the opening of *Things Fall Apart* when we were brought into an immediate, intimate relationship with a traditional, pre-colonial African clan, by means of Achebe's authoritative and yet sympathetic, unpatronizing narratorial voice. But consider the first page of *In a Free State*. Even before we read the opening words, there is something unexpected about what appears to be the start of a novel. In place of the usual chapter number or title, or even a simple blank above the prose, we have 'Prologue, from a Journal'. A prologue – as an introductory speech addressed to the audience directly – is familiar from drama; it is a kind of introduction that is simultaneously part of the main work. If you turn a page back, you'll find (does Naipaul expect first-time readers to notice?) that the contents list is also unusual, with – instead of chapters – several headings, the first and last of which are distinguished from the rest by being italicized.

5.13 So the prologue and epilogue provide some sort of frame for the three headings between them, a frame which, it is implied, is different in quality or importance from the intermediate material, and yet part of it. Perhaps the word 'Journal' will help us go further? Presumably here it means a factual (possibly daily) personal account of, for example, someone's travels. What do we then get? A title, 'The Tramp at Piraeus', followed by fourteen pages of narrative. Let's consider this narrative.

ACTIVITY

Please now re-read up to page 20, and answer the following:

(a) In what sense is this a journal?

(b) Who or what is the tramp?

(c) What makes him the focus of this first piece of narrative?

(d) What is the predominant narrative technique?

(e) What is the story – if that is what it is – about?

(f) What theme(s) do you think are suggested or introduced by this first section of the narrative?

(The questions are obviously linked, but keep them separate if possible.)

SAMPLE ANSWER

(a) This is a journal only in a rather attenuated sense, of having a first-person narrator recounting an incident witnessed during his travels.

(b) The 'tramp' in question is an eccentric, frail and elderly Englishman travelling alone on a crowded steamer during a two-day journey from Piraeus to Alexandria.

(c) He is the focus partly because of what happens, partly because of who is describing it. The tramp arouses the fascination but also the anger of several fellow-passengers. Some unspecified overnight misdemeanour leads the three men sharing his cabin to gang up on, tease and provoke him, until 'the game' and the trip come to an end. All this is observed with interest by one of the other passengers.

(d) This passenger is the 'I' of the story, the narrator. He is himself the fascinated yet detached observer of what happens to the tramp. The originating voice is first-person, from within the narrative, but the perspective is authoritative, non-participatory; almost, but not quite, omniscient.

(e) The story is about the temporary relationships between people thrown together – from different parts of the world, or belonging to different cultures and races – while on board ship.

(f) The preceding point relates to the question of theme(s). Home and homelessness; power and powerlessness, seem obvious themes. But if you think of the book's title, you are taken a step further. All the characters are in some sense 'free' – free of their countries, their roots, even simply their usual securities.

DISCUSSION

Although we might well have expected a 'prologue' to address us directly, and although the journal-narrator does use the first-person pronoun, what we have is a short narrative account of an event witnessed, an anecdote. If we recall the book's title, it does appear as if the prologue introduces one major theme of the story. This is the question of 'freedom', of what it means to be free (in different but related senses of the word) – free to return to a place, like the refugees, free to travel, like the businessmen and tourists, free to speak your mind and to behave eccentrically, like the English tramp; except that he isn't really free, is he? He ends up locking himself in his cabin to avoid his three persecutors.

All of which prompts the question: are the freedoms of the characters compromised in some way? If so, is this compromise a matter of individual states of mind, or history or politics? Or all of these? What about the freedom of Egypt?

ACTIVITY

You may well have noticed that there are specific verbal echoes of the book's title running through the prologue. What is their function? Consider the fourth paragraph in particular: who or what were 'the invaders'? And what do you make of the phrase, 'the casualties of that freedom'?

SAMPLE ANSWER/DISCUSSION

These echoes alert us to the prologue's function of introducing the book's themes. The fourth paragraph is the most explicit. The bulk of the passengers on the overcrowded little steamer

> were Egyptian Greeks. They were travelling to Egypt, but Egypt was no longer their home. They had been expelled; they were refugees. The invaders had left Egypt; after many humiliations Egypt was free; and these Greeks, the poor ones, who by simple skills had made themselves only just less poor than Egyptians, were the casualties of that freedom.
>
> (pp.7–8)

Who are, or rather were, 'the invaders'? The British: this was published less than two decades after the Suez crisis. (The failure of the British and their allies to defeat Egypt in 1956 was a clearer signal of the end of imperial power than the victory of Indian nationalism in 1947.) We quickly realize that it is typical of the narrator's economic, elliptical and indirect manner to adopt for the moment the term that those he is talking about would have used – this is part of what gives the narration its omniscient feel, although it is first-person. To the Egyptians, the British colonizers were the invaders who humiliated them – doubly so, by going on to try to control the country long after granting it formal independence. Using the generalized term 'invaders' has a further resonance; it reminds us that this is a country which has seen other invaders, other empires – the French before the British, for example, and the Turks before them. Hence, 'many humiliations'.

And yet in the decolonized, 'free' Egypt not everyone has become free. Certainly not the Greek workers, who were forced to flee, 'the casualties of that freedom', and who are now returning – with what hope?

The phrase describing them as 'the casualties of that freedom' is crucial, because of the clear implication that freedom has its losers as well as its winners, and because it highlights the fact that the whole of this opening narrative has to do with the losses rather than the gains of freedom. This is even the case for the former rulers, isn't it? British power as it is represented here, in the tramp, is not just on the wane, it is in pathetic tatters. It is notable, and anticipates the structure and method of the entire book, that the different 'casualties' of freedom are in different positions – individual, social, political – and are represented in different ways. Nor are we drawn into the same level or quality of sympathy for each of them: the tramp is individualized more as a character, which helps gain more sympathetic attention for him, whereas the refugees below deck are quite another matter. Look at the last paragraph on page 19, in which we return to them as they are about to re-enter Egypt. They are described coming up from the lower deck, with the

> slack bodies and bad skins of people who ate too many carbohydrates. Their blotched faces were immobile, distant, but full of a fierce, foolish cunning. They were watching.
>
> (p.19)

Hardly sympathetic; on the contrary, it is stereotyping the refugees as an anonymous, barely human and frightening 'other'. Yet – and we will come back to this strategy again later, when considering Naipaul's 'racism' – the little detail about their diet makes for an ambiguous response, since we aren't allowed simply to dislike them, but are made to realize simultaneously that there is a reason why they may appear repellent to an observer on the upper deck. This observer, we might also have noticed, has described himself as fearful of being involved with what he sees going on around him (see the top of page 12), which undermines his position a little, too. Is he also some kind of casualty?

5.14 What I'm trying to suggest is twofold: firstly, to understand what's going on, we must attend to quite subtle detail in the narration; and secondly, since this is all within the prologue, it must anticipate the main body of the book in technique as well as in theme. Further, if you recall that according to the contents list there is an epilogue, also 'from a Journal', we would expect that concluding part of the book to have some kind of relationship with this part. As it happens, the epilogue also concerns the narrator arriving in Egypt (although from Italy, not Greece). In both instances, therefore, he is travelling from what used to be a peak of European culture (underlined by his observation of the liner *Leonardo da Vinci* as their ship leaves Piraeus) to the source of a far older civilization. And Egypt is in a sense the centrepoint of the cultures of the world: Europe to the north, the Orient to the east, Africa to the south, and – last, by no means least – America to the west. All these other places, the origins of ancient and modern empires (including, in the epilogue, the Chinese), are touched on in the book. Another telling little detail in the prologue hints at which empire now prevails, however: the entire ship is held up at the start of its journey because 'some of the American schoolchildren had gone ashore to buy food' (p.8). These children are shown to be quite indifferent to what happens to their fellow passengers, gazing out to sea as the little drama concerning the English tramp takes place.

5.15   So this is a book about empires, and about what happens as one empire comes to an end and another begins. It is also about what happens to individuals caught up in these large movements of history, their struggles (generally futile) to be free. The focus of the opening section is on a member of the most recent empire to decline, the British. In this context, it is a particularly rich irony that this man should say, after a brief account of his travels around the world (all to former British colonies), 'what's nationality these days? I myself, I think of myself as a citizen of the world' (p.9). One of several layers of irony in this boast in the post-imperial period is that it alludes to earlier times, when British culture and society were growing in power and respect around the world and 'English gentlemen' travelled abroad secure in the knowledge of their country's 'superiority'. This is clear even if we do not recognize the origins of the phrase 'citizen of the world', which alludes to Oliver Goldsmith's eighteenth-century satire upon the English, in which a sophisticated Chinaman provided a nicely critical outsider's view of his host's customs and peculiarities. (Goldsmith got his title from Sir Francis Bacon, who remarked in one of his famous essays that 'if a man be gracious and courteous to strangers, it shows he is a citizen of the world'.)

5.16   A further irony is that it is Naipaul himself, the Asian cosmopolite diarist-writer, who is claiming the authority to comment upon the customs and peculiarities of others in the prologue and, by implication, throughout the book. Only in the epilogue does he come before us in person, however; elsewhere he is behind, above or beyond his narrators, paring his nails. We will return to the function of the epilogue. What should be clear is the function of the prologue. It is not to 'set the scene' in a conventional sense: the scene, character and narration change immediately after the prologue, in a way that (if you aren't expecting it from the contents list) is astounding; and this change is followed by another, and another. Instead, the prologue introduces certain themes, most obviously that of the struggles of displaced individuals in the post-colonial world. 'Struggles' may be an understatement, if we think of the easy cruelty towards the tramp of those other, more powerful 'citizens of the world' – the Lebanese furniture-maker, the Egyptian student, and Hans, the 'well-developed' young Austrian. As the narrator comments:

> It was to be like a tiger-hunt, where bait is laid out and the hunter and spectators watch from the security of a platform. The bait here was the tramp's own rucksack.
>
> (p.15)

And so, a final twist: the Englishman is to be tormented in a way reminiscent of an old imperial pastime of the British, hunting tiger in India, on the backs of elephants. The contrast with the preceding novel in this block, *Things Fall Apart*, couldn't be stronger: with *In a Free State*, we have an allusive, ironic, indirect (in short, Modernist) narrative which deals with the contemporary, post-colonial world and characters from a multitude of backgrounds, the whole resonating with large historical movements, the rise and fall of empires.

The search for identity

5.17   The way in which we read the new writings depends on the 'production' and status of the author just as much as (if not more than) it does when we read the more familiar 'canon'. The new writings are not so 'new' anymore, and their themes have been identified and packaged to a surprising extent already. This puts peculiar pressures on authors who are institutionalized in this way. Reviewing a collection of academic papers on Commonwealth literature, over twenty years ago, Naipaul ruefully noted the appearance of 'occasional references to myself', and continued:

> Things move so fast nowadays, even in the Literature Schools.
> Commonwealth writing as we understand it is so new, and already it is
> being picked to pieces … it all seems to have been codified already … Then
> there is the West Indian with his search for identity. Here is a phrase that
> has gone deep. Students, already – how disquieting! – preparing theses,
> write or even telephone to say that they get the impression from my books
> that I am engaged in a search for identity. How is it going? At times like
> this I am glad to be only a name.
>
> (Naipaul, 1965)

5.18   Yet the theme of 'identity' is unavoidable in any discussion of Caribbean writing, and Naipaul's work, including *In a Free State*, is no exception. As Gareth Griffiths has pointed out,

> the force with which the educational and social myths of borrowed identity
> have split the West Indian from his own reality … is not the invention of
> tortured intellectuals but an overwhelming and continuous pressure
> experienced by all classes and groups within West Indian society.
>
> (Griffiths, 1978, p.106)

There are, however, radically different ways of responding to this split, including attempts to accept one's fractured inheritance, to return and rediscover one's society, one's place – even to look ahead, as Derek Walcott does, to a fusion of the fragments into a heterogeneous local culture of the future. Naipaul's writings display a different response, pervaded as they are by an overwhelming sense of personal dislocation, apparently defeating any potential reconstruction of the personality, the self, in some future Caribbean culture. Each of Naipaul's narratives – whether autobiography, documentary or fiction – seems to represent another attempt to discover or establish the sense of self that eludes him and that, he insists, eludes the colonial subject from the Caribbean, if not all colonial peoples: 'Living in a borrowed culture, the West Indian, more than most, needs writers to tell him who he is and where he stands', he observed in *The Middle Passage* (p.73).

5.19   Naipaul's most persuasive attempt to do this was embodied in *A House for Mr Biswas* (completed just before he wrote those words), where the central character aspires towards the secure identity that he feels a house of his own would give him; but it ends with his dying in a jerry-built wreck which, despite the 'romantic aspect' provided by his laburnum tree, destroys him through debt and despair. Mr Biswas's failure, underlined by the use (again) of a framing prologue and epilogue, leaves the inescapable conclusion that all such attempts at redefinition in the colonial context are illusory. The reasons for this view are not hard to find. Again and again Naipaul describes the societies of the Caribbean in terms of lack. The Trinidad of his childhood, 'too unimportant' and peripheral a country to have a history, and with a society based on slavery, exploitation and crass materialism, left

> everyone [as] an individual, fighting for his place in the community. Yet
> there was no community. We were of various races, religions, sets and
> cliques; and we had somehow found ourselves on the same small island.

Nothing bound us together except this common residence. There was no nationalist feeling; there could be none. There was no profound anti-imperialist feeling; indeed, it was only our Britishness, our belonging to the British Empire, which gave us any identity.

(*The Middle Passage*, 1969b, p.45)

5.20   The position is paradoxical: Naipaul himself goes on, again and again, to try to uncover the supposedly non-existent history of his place, his culture; and, in *The Middle Passage*, while insisting that the West Indies 'are so completely a creation of Empire that the withdrawal of Empire is almost without meaning', he is also at times prepared to admit that in such a situation 'nationalism is the only revitalizing force'. But that is in British Guiana – to which troops were dispatched to destroy the radical nationalism of the early fifties – just as in Notting Hill, London, when assertion turned to riot, 'the energy which, already gathered, ought to have gone towards an ordered and overdue social revolution was dissipated in racial rivalry, factional strife and simple fear' (*The Middle Passage*, p.153).

5.21   And so we end up where we were before. The futility of communal, *political* action, no matter how necessary, is a constant theme; and Naipaul simply cannot conceive of an individual gaining a sense of identity from the common cause. We are always left with isolated individuals, without a community, circling back upon themselves.

5.22   But what about Naipaul's own 'race, religion, clique', the rural Hindu community? Vidiahar Surajprasad Naipaul was in fact born (17 August 1932) in Chaguanas, a small market town in the heart of the sugar-cane area of Trinidad, and was the grandson of indentured labourers of Brahmin descent – i.e. of the highest or priestly caste in the Hindu socio-religious system. As a young man he could understand, but not speak, Hindi, developing a Brahmin delicacy about cooking and personal habits while resisting Hindu belief and ritual. He belonged from the start, then, to a particular subculture within the multicultural, multiracial, multilayered society of his island colony, a subculture permeated with a sense of difference. At first this sounds as though it provides a refuge:

> Everything which made the Indian alien in the society gave him strength. His alienness insulated him from the black–white struggle. He was taboo-ridden as no other person on the island: he had complicated rules about food and about what was unclean. His religion gave him values which were not the white values of the rest of the community, and preserved him from self-contempt; he never lost pride in his origins. More important than religion was his family organization, an enclosing self-sufficient world absorbed with its quarrels and jealousies, as difficult for the outsider to penetrate as for one of its members to escape. It protected and imprisoned, a static world, awaiting decay.

(*The Middle Passage*, p.88)

5.23   By its religion, its alternative system of values, this community is protected from succumbing wholesale to the dominant, colonial, white values, and hence from the 'self-contempt' of those who have, according to Naipaul, had such alternatives erased by the historic experience of the middle passage. But if his community protects, it also imprisons; and Naipaul admits his own overwhelming urge to escape it. On the other hand, members of the community retain an identity: 'he never lost pride in his origins.' If Indian and African alike have been left in a void by the processes of history, the Indian can at least grasp the root of an earlier, identifiable culture. Naipaul escapes Trinidad (the first time at 18, on an 'island scholarship' to Oxford); he returns on visits (the first time at 24, after graduation, marriage and a job at the BBC); but he also goes to India for a year, to the very village from which his grandfather migrated to Trinidad; and he returns, again and again, to

India. What does he seek? His identity. What does he find? The titles of the books he has written about the country and its attitudes suggest what he thinks he finds – *An Area of Darkness* (1968), *India: a wounded civilization* (1977), and *India: a million mutinies now* (1990). As he admits early in the first account:

> even now, though time has widened, though space has contracted and I have travelled lucidly over that area which was to me [as a child] the area of darkness, something of darkness remains, in those attitudes, those ways of thinking and seeing, which are no longer mine.
>
> (*An Area of Darkness*, 1968, p.30)

It is a darkness he continues to explore:

> but increasingly I understand that my Indian memories, the memories of that India which lived on into my childhood in Trinidad, are like trapdoors into a bottomless past.
>
> (*India: a wounded civilization*, 1979, p.10)

5.24   The identity is unreachable, in other words. Even when, as in the third Indian book, he sets out to introduce 'people who have ideas now of who they are and what they are themselves', he himself cannot relate to them, he withdraws. His failure to settle in India has brought with it from the start the realization that what he finds – instead of a land of achievement based on a whole, living and long-standing traditional culture – is another fractured, or at least 'wounded', culture lost in a 'double fantasy', a mixture of mimicry of the West and oriental resignation, stasis (*An Area of Darkness*, pp.216–17). He compares his search for an identity with a piece of patterned cloth unwoven to trace the figures, which ends up a heap of tangled threads (ibid., p.266). The image is doubly suggestive: of personal frustration at the inevitable outcome of his search for a common identity; and of the tangle of differing narrative forms in which he represents that frustration, that search. In *In a Free State*, that tangle becomes part of the very texture of the book, in which Trinidad and India feature as points of contact, of questioning, rather than as either home or destination.

5.25   The search for identity is evident in the first story after the prologue of *In a Free State*, 'One out of Many', which takes us from Bombay to Washington. The title suggests multiple ironies: it is a play on the motto of the USA, *E pluribus unum*, and the familiar American notion that everyone can become an American; it also reminds us of US hegemony in the world, hinted at in the prologue; and it anticipates the ironic contrast between Western individualism and Hindu communalism which runs through the story. If we are tempted to think that the 'I' at the beginning is the same as the narrator of the journal, we are quickly made aware that this cannot be so. In any case, comparing the opening sentences with the opening of the prologue reveals a quite distinct tone and syntax: in place of that earlier sophisticated, detached and ironic tone, and complex syntax, we have here a simpler 'confessional' mode:

> I am now an American citizen and I live in Washington, capital of the world. Many people, both here and in India, will feel that I have done well. But.
>
> (p.21)

5.26   That 'But' alerts us to the potential for undermining, ironic reversal that follows. We are at the heart of the new empire, aspired to by many; and significantly, in the light of what we know about Naipaul's own struggle to come to terms with his Indian identity, the Indian central character's predicament is a provocative and sympathetic reversal of his own. Instead of the Westernized and insecure former colonial from the New World coming to ancient India, here is an Indian of India, secure in his own culture and beliefs, part of the crowd on a Bombay street, coming to the New World. What happens to him? What does he see?

ACTIVITY

To answer these questions involves getting to grips with the new development of narrative adopted here. I've called it confessional, but there's more to it than that. What kind of narrative is it? Re-read to the top of page 27, the end of the first subsection that concludes with Santosh's arrival in the Washington apartment. Do you detect humour here? To what end is it directed?

SAMPLE ANSWER/DISCUSSION

This is another kind of journal, isn't it? First-person, direct discourse, but instead of the 'I' as a witness, hardly participating in his account, this is the 'I' as teller of his own tale; indeed, everything is viewed from his perspective, and it seems to be very much the point that we realize this is a limited perspective, quite unlike the omniscient prologue.

Furthermore, it is not just humour, but more like *satire*, isn't it? As with all the other segments of narrative in the book, it involves a journey; but this is the journey of an innocent abroad, a traditional satire subject from *Candide* to *Huckleberry Finn*. The narrator's attempts to apply the simple values of his Hindu background on the Air India flight go farcically wrong, as he swallows the betel juice he isn't allowed to spit, unknowingly sips champagne and ends up vomiting over his bundles. He is that familiar satirical figure, the simpleton who fails to come to grips with reality and suffers accordingly, but whose adventures show up his moral, if not spiritual, superiority to those he encounters. Naipaul expressed disgust at the ubiquitous evidence of casual excretion he found in India. Here it is the hysterical cabin steward (when she is disgusted with her compatriot's physical habits) who is made to look absurd, not the frightened man who cannot control himself in the 'tiny hissing room' at the back of the aircraft. The humour is light, and at the expense of the 'civilized', whether Indian or American:

> 'He's a cook,' my employer said.
>
> 'Does he always travel with his condiments?'
>
> (p.26)

This exchange becomes analeptically even more amusing when we realize, later, that the US customs officials have missed what else Santosh has brought into the country: 'the poor country weed I smoked' (p.34). His simplicity helps him to survive; but at what cost? Formerly 'free' to stroll on the Bombay streets, enjoying the 'respect and security' shed upon him by the importance of his employer (for all his dependence on the man), he now finds himself in a place where a 'wild race' roams the streets 'so freely', while he is 'like a prisoner' under the 'imitation sky' in the corridor of his master's apartment block (pp.26–7).

As we proceed with Santosh's account of his journey of self-discovery, the irony of his position becomes more complex, if bleaker. His development towards the 'freedom' he desires – leaving domestic employment, finding more independent work, marrying to legalize himself as a US citizen – is marked by a series of telling little moments, sometimes comic, sometimes pathetic, but all tending to the conclusion that his freedom (the word itself is kept in play throughout) is an illusion. But it is an illusion of which he is aware, unlike those he meets. The added irony develops as we are brought to realize that this is 60s America – the time of hippies, black urban riots, and a popular youth culture of the Orient, with different groups aspiring towards their idea of freedom, all set in the critical perspective implied by Santosh's condition, the condition of the colonial immigrant.

To begin with, this means that it is others who are shown to be living an illusion. The hippies and their specious Orientalism make him wonder if

> perhaps once upon a time they had been like me ... brought here among
> the *hubshi* as captives a long time ago and [who] had become a lost people,
> like our own wandering gipsy folk, and had forgotten who they were.
>
> (p.30)

This wonderfully ironic fantasy makes them seem, with their bad Sanskrit and odd dancing, 'something that should be kin but turns out not to be, turns out to be degraded, like a deformed man, or like a leper, who from a distance looks whole' (p.30). Their lack of identity is like a disease to Santosh, in his own insecurity. The entire white American world outside seems unreal: 'Americans have remained to me, as people not quite real, as people temporarily absent from television' (p.33); while the black American world of the streets is all too real, so that when the *hubshi*, as he calls them, try to burn down Washington, he wants his own block to burn, 'even myself', to be destroyed and consumed (p.40).

ACTIVITY

It has been suggested that this is 'an intensely racist story', in that Santosh's 'liberation' is sketched against a background of stereotyped black people, whose activities are indicated as 'lost' and 'make-believe' (Cudjoe, 1988, p.146). Would you agree? Is the story racist? Consider what happens when he wanders around the smoking ruins of the city:

> they smiled at me and I found I was smiling back. Happiness was on the
> faces of the *hubshi*. They were like people amazed they could do so much,
> that so much lay in their power. They were like people on holiday. I shared
> their exhilaration.
>
> (p.41)

DISCUSSION

This feeling of exhilaration is what enables Santosh to escape from his employer. It's of course true that black power has been expressed destructively, in the burning of the city. But I don't myself quite see Naipaul's attitude as racist. Not only does the narrator's response acknowledge a kinship (unlike his response to white Americans), which can be interpreted as acknowledging the oppression of black Americans, a colonial people within the metropolitan state and also struggling to achieve a sense of identity. But it is through the interest shown by a black American woman, and not by his fellow Indian expatriates, that he achieves even the dubious status that allows him to stay where he is.

It is arguable that the presentation of the black servant he marries to obtain citizenship is racist – and sexist. Her otherness is stressed, and the narrator's attempt to naturalize it only demeans her further: she is large and threatening, the incarnation of Kali, the black Hindu goddess of destruction (pp.38, 53); furthermore, 'It is written in our books, both holy and not so holy, that it is indecent and wrong for a man of our blood to embrace the *hubshi* woman. To be dishonoured in this life, to be born a cat or a monkey or a *hubshi* in the next!' (pp.34–5).

But Kali's other aspect is of creation, and there is more than a hint of ironic humour in the presentation of Santosh's Hindu fastidiousness, as he succumbs to the *hubshi's* vitality, and her difference from himself. She was also, after all, the first to teach him English ('Me black and beautiful' and 'He pig', p.34) and helps create the self-awareness that enables him to break out of his servitude. Yet that 'freedom' leaves him, consistent with the rest of the book, a 'casualty'. Does this thematic, structuring pressure rob the conclusion of conviction?

It depends, I think, on what you make of the concluding paragraph. Santosh was once 'part of the flow'; all that his freedom has brought him 'is the knowledge that I have a face and have a body, that I must feed this body and clothe this body for a certain number of years. Then it will be over' (p.58). The last word echoes the last word of the book's prologue: 'That passion was over' (p.20). A certain Hindu submissiveness is all that remains, it seems. From an author who claims to have left Hinduism behind in childhood, and finds its manifestations in India dubious and constricting, this engagement with its ideology is something of a surprise. Elsewhere, Naipaul argues that Western European and US attempts to enter 'Hindu equilibrium' may be possible for scholars, at the level of 'intellectual comprehension'; but to try to enter it as a 'reality' is another matter. 'The hippies of Western Europe and United States' give the illusion of having done so; but 'they break just at the point where the Hindu begins: the knowledge of the abyss, the acceptance of distress as the condition of men' (1977, p.27). Is this the knowledge towards which *In a Free State* is tending?

The post-colonial narrative

5.27 *In a Free State* explores the shifting and ambiguous relationship between the developed West and the Third World. As we read on through the sequence of seemingly disconnected narratives, it becomes increasingly apparent that they involve a progressive narrative exploration of this fundamental 'story', and of its implications for the predicament of individuals caught up in the network of forces – social, political, historical and economic – that the story reveals. In particular, we see the painful illusion of freedom that continues to grip them. A full exploration demands that we experience the perspective of the colonial, or rather ex-colonial, masters themselves, and in the title-story, also the longest narrative, the earlier perspective on immigration and exile is reversed, as two members of the dominant metropolitan culture and former empire journey through an independent African state.

5.28 But, as Naipaul went on to admit in *The Enigma of Arrival* (1987), his most autobiographical 'novel' so far, when writing *In a Free State* the Africa of his imagination 'was not only the source countries – Kenya, Uganda, the Congo, Rwanda; it was also Trinidad, to which I had gone back with a vision of romance and had seen black men with threatening hair' (p.157). If a certain impossible dream of his Indian roots is perceptible in the second sequence of the book, another vision, this time a nightmare from his Trinidadian home, emerges in the third, as if it has to be confronted explicitly before it becomes part of the 'African' title-story. The book *In a Free State* is like a palimpsest, a series of fragmentary layers, through which we can perceive from time to time, as we peel them off, what lies beneath. It may be that, in the end, this makes it more, rather than less, representative of the history and culture of Naipaul's origin – multilayered, multifarious and impossible to reduce to the experience of one nation, place or people.

ACTIVITY

Please now read 'Tell Me Who to Kill', comparing it with 'One out of Many'. What is the basic similarity? What is the basic difference? What do you make of the narrator's state of mind? Can his version of events be relied on? Finally, do you notice any aspects of popular culture used to mediate the experiences of the narrator?

SAMPLE ANSWER/DISCUSSION

Here we have, once again, the predicament of the colonial who has journeyed to the metropolitan centre, seeking freedom but finding the imprisonment of exile. A step ahead of Santosh, the moment he embarks upon his journey he feels like a prisoner, he 'will never be a free man again' (p.79). His story is told entirely in his voice and from his perspective; but this time he is West Indian and so, according to Naipaul's view, *already* deracinated. And whereas Santosh mildly accepts what he understands as fate handing out to him homelessness and isolation, the *anonymous* narrator here responds to what happens to him (and, another difference, to his brothers) out of an inner potential for disorder and violence. His brother Dayo's marriage to a white girl provides an analogy to Santosh's marriage; but this wedding is like a funeral, and the narrator feels he is already 'the dead man' (p.102).

This destructive potential is evident from the moment we encounter the fractured, obsessive and frightening narrative consciousness. It is hard to know how far – or in what sense – we can rely on this man's account of what is going on around him. His paranoia is signalled by, for example, the contradictory accounts of Frank as a friend and comforter on the one hand, and as someone who exposes him to pain, even challenges him to become violent, on the other. In contrast to Santosh's home life, his early experiences in the colony (Trinidad is implied, not named) have practically severed his sense of belonging to any viable culture. Occasional hints of a Hindu background ('No turban, no procession, no drums...' at the wedding, p.99) serve only to increase the feeling that he finds himself robbed of any sense of self-worth, of identity. He has been aware since before he leaves 'how ordinary the world was for me, with nothing good in it, nothing to see except sugarcane and the pitch road, and how from small I know I had no life' (p.64). His understanding of himself and the world is rendered in a distinctive Caribbean creole voice, which, far from allowing us to celebrate its vital and popular origins, is used to signal further the humiliating inadequacy that prompts his anger.

More striking yet are the fragments of 40s American film culture, imperfectly recollected, which dominate his consciousness, and which Naipaul has elsewhere registered as characteristic of the city life of his childhood. At an earlier stage Naipaul exploited the richness and humour of Trinidadian popular culture and everyday speech, even while he bewailed its limitations, its secondhandness. It's worth briefly noting the contradictory elements in his position: the sentence that, according to his own account (1984, p.16), initiated his writing career, included the dialect utterance 'What happening there, Bogart?' This 'Port of Spain memory' developed as the central, poignant thread running through his first book (but third to be published), *Miguel Street* (1959). In part a celebration of his Port of Spain experiences (the Naipaul family moved there when he was six), the stories collected in *Miguel Street* also dramatized the frustrating meanness of small-town colonial life. Its cast of characters, from B. Wordsworth ('"B" for Black. White Wordsworth was my brother. We share one heart') to Bogart the bigamist (named after the wildly popular Hollywood 'tough guy'), were depicted with increasing detachment by a young boy, the narrator whose consciousness links the stories, and who determines to leave the limited world of colonial Trinidad at the end, observing only 'my shadow before me, a dancing dwarf on the tarmac'.

And so only mimicry or parody remain for the departed colonial, doubly deceived in that he imitates an imitation of an imitation, Hollywood in the tropics. Many other West Indian writers have dealt with the predicament of the immigrant in London in terms of the unfriendly natives, unfriendly climate; 'Tell Me Who to Kill' shows all this, and white racism, but the central image is that threatening fantasy/dream image from Hitchcock's *Rope*, of the body in the chest (p.62), to which the narrator returns in his last words (p.102), leaving us unclear about whether or not there *has* been a killing, but certain that there *will* be. You need to know about the film to appreciate the reference more fully in this context. *Rope* (1948) was set in the USA, and was based on the Leopold and Loeb murders: in the film version, two homosexual boys murder a fellow-student for 'kicks' and serve his relatives a meal from a chest containing the body. There are hints of a suppressed, disturbed sexuality in the relationship between the narrator and Frank (pp.59–60, 64), suggesting that the narrator may be a sexual 'casualty of freedom' as well. This anticipates the characterization of the central character of the succeeding narrative, Bobby, whose reasons for living in the newly independent African state are at least partly bound up with a struggle to find sexual freedom.

But the precise reason for the breakdown of the narrator in 'Tell Me Who to Kill' is not made quite clear. Or rather, the main point seems to lie elsewhere, in the arbitrariness of the assault at its centre and the conscious and unconscious collusion of all those involved. What Naipaul is suggesting here (perhaps not wholly successfully, though) is that the colonized subject becomes a seething mass of unfocused anger: who, indeed, to kill, when your condition has been brought about by such large, incomprehensible forces? No wonder, then, that so much of the hatred is directed inwards, or at those nearest, his own people, since there are no *individuals* to blame. The colonizers have in any case departed: there is little to be gained by threatening the English 'louts' who provoke him in the roti-shop; indeed, it is this momentary surge of power that leaves him feeling 'dead'. In place of the colonizers there are now the 'neo-colonials', like Bobby and Linda, in the long title-story. The hatred and violence they witness is also directed mainly by the colonized towards each other. But there is more to it than that.

ACTIVITY

Let's turn to the title-story, which you should now re-read. First, try summing up in a paragraph what it is about. Then, consider the question: what kind of narrative is it? The shift of gear is immediately apparent, as it has been with each of the preceding narratives in the sequence, so the opening page (103) will reveal how this new narrative voice sounds.

SAMPLE ANSWER/DISCUSSION

The title-story or novella is set in a recently independent or 'free' African state during a period of civil unrest. It follows the journey of two white English expatriates – the homosexual civil servant Bobby, and the adulterous colonial wife Linda – as they travel by car from the capital through a changing landscape and set of experiences to the shelter of a government compound. Bobby, the main character, we first see humiliated when he makes an advance towards a black South African exile; then, finally, he is beaten up when he tries to pacify an African soldier. Linda has to face both the rejection of a suitor who is following them, and Bobby's antagonism. Their escape to the compound only confirms the inadequacy of both Bobby's liberal, pro-African stance and Linda's pragmatic-colonialism. The story concludes with Bobby taking on the role of the white master. As for the way it is told ('In this country in Africa there was a president and there was also a king. They belonged to different tribes. The enmity of the tribes was old...'), surely this resembles the voice of a traditional or 'folk' tale? And yet, very quickly, the voice modulates to a more familiar, authoritative, third-person narrator, doesn't it? As the focus narrows during 'this week of crisis', with Bobby in the capital attending a seminar on 'development' while a civil war grows, so too does the irony develop. In the capital, with its half-acre gardens 'in what was still an English suburb', 'there was no sign of war or crisis'. That is to be found in the 'wilderness', beyond even the 'bush villages' that tourists visit for souvenirs.

It is clear from the first page that yet another new terrain is being mapped out here: a former colonial capital still much as it was, the embodiment of a certain genteel, imported conception of order, of Englishness, and the growing, anarchic forces at large in the recently decolonized country. As in any narrative, we are evidently being invited to develop a set of meanings from this opening; but what is unexpected, even after the variety of narrative styles we have met in this sequence, is that the starting-point is an almost mythic, symbolic realm. Why is it like that? And why the shift into a more 'traditional', realist mode as well? Are we being alerted to earlier forms of narrative, especially earlier forms of narrating the colonial encounter? It would appear so. As critics have pointed out, Conrad's *Heart of Darkness* is especially close here, and there is an important sense in which 'In a Free State' is a comment on, and development of, that classic colonial text.

5.29 We've already come across *Heart of Darkness* in relation to *Things Fall Apart* (see Section 2) to make the point that Achebe's novel overturns the characteristically European perspective upon the 'otherness' of African peoples embodied in texts such as Conrad's. But 'In a Free State' suggests a much more specific connection – indeed, at one point, on page 161, Bobby tells Linda, 'You've been reading too much Conrad. I hate that book, don't you?' Do you recall the context of his remark? It is after Linda has observed a group of Africans in brightly coloured gowns walking past them in the rain: 'I feel that sort of forest life has been going on forever.' Her observation is one of a series of references to the existence of some kind of primeval Africa, predating colonialism, and going back to earlier empires. The question is, how are we to respond to them?

5.30 On one level, what Linda says appears simply as a typical colonial-expatriate reflex, that 'Kenya-settler' romanticism of the 'pre-man side of Africa' which Bobby sneers at in her (p.119), and which anyone familiar with, say (one of the best of the genre), Karen Blixen's *Out of Africa* (1937) would easily recognize. Emphasizing the 'primitive' and 'timeless' in Africa appeals to Europeans made insecure by the larger changes in their world, such as the loss of empire, and enables them to patronize the African people even when they have gained their independence ('Poor little king', Linda remarks elsewhere, p.135).

5.31 But to understand the specific allusion, and to see the point of the Conradian echoes that reverberate through the story, we need to turn for a moment to 'that book', *Heart of Darkness*, itself. *Heart of Darkness* is an account of a journey into the 'heart' of an unnamed African country, told from the perspective of the colonizers. Marlow, the teller of the tale to an anonymous narrator, is himself sceptical of the colonial enterprise. Marlow's search for Mr Kurtz – the company agent whose commercial dealings with the 'natives' have taken him beyond the bounds of 'civilized' if not human behaviour – is described in terms simultaneously suggestive of an exotic adventure, a critique of imperialism, and a semi-allegoric or parabolic exploration of the psyche. Although based on the author's experience of the Belgian exploitation of the Congo in the early 1890s, Conrad's narrative is made geographically and historically unspecific – replacing Matadi, Kinshasa and Stanley Falls on the Congo with the 'Company Station', the 'Central Station' and the 'Inner Station', and also avoiding proper names by referring to 'pilgrims', 'savages', 'the Manager' and so on.

5.32   It's pretty clear that the element of moral fable implicit in the opening of 'In a Free State' is only the first of a series of Conradian echoes and parallels. Naipaul, too, involves his colonial characters in an emblematic journey away from the Europeanized world towards an increasingly challenging 'primitive' Africa: from the unnamed capital through rainforest, mountain, plain and savannah, stopping along the way at run-down colonial outposts such as the Hunting Lodge or the colonel's hotel, until finally, in the Southern Collectorate, they get to the ruined palace of the murdered king. The further south Bobby and Linda go, the more they reveal the illusions and self-deceptions of the white expatriates they represent – although, unlike Conrad's Marlow, neither of them appears to gain any self-knowledge as a result. Instead, their own prejudices and inadequacies emerge more and more clearly until, in the heat of the moment, they become hostile, even vicious towards each other and so, inevitably, towards the Africans upon whom they project their inner disorder.

5.33   Order and disorder, power and powerlessness, freedom and its lack, continue to occupy the book's narrative development. Thus, Bobby's angry response to Linda's account of her confused and frightened arrival in the country is 'You came for the freedom, though', which in turn drives her to exclaim: 'You should either stay away, or you should go among them with the whip in your hand' (p.218). This is after their relationship has gone through various stages, from irritation to affection, from compassion to hatred. But at this point Linda's statement alerts us to, and brings back into range, Conrad's vision of colonialism as something that can push those who participate in it towards violent extremes. In *Heart of Darkness*, the idealist Kurtz ends up exclaiming 'Exterminate the brutes' (Conrad, 1971 edn, p.51). Violence, or the threat of it, accompanies Bobby and Linda throughout, just as in Conrad's novella the possibility of sudden death lurks around every bend in the river. Here, whether it is the '*yak-yak-yak*' of the helicopter overhead, or the overweight soldiers jogging under an Israeli instructor, the colonel waiting to be murdered by his staff, the wild dogs roaming the streets, or just the sudden sharp changes in the road or the weather, there is a pervasive sense of threat, to the extent that it feels like a condition of life. In other words, as in *Heart of Darkness*, the pressure of a symbolic, or representative, level of narrative discourse seems unavoidable.

5.34   And so if, like Conrad's Congo, Naipaul's 'free state' is based on known places and events, it also seeks a kind of symbolic autonomy. Landeg White describes this well; the main story, he says, is 'sufficiently located in recent history to seem real, and sufficiently generalized to seem representative' (1975, p.196). The politics of Naipaul's story are those of Uganda in May 1966 when the Kabaka of Buganda (or 'King Freddie', as he was known alike overseas and to the expatriate community) was overthrown by the Prime Minister, Milton Obote, who controlled the army. But the allusions to oath-taking refer to Kenya and the Mau Mau, while the disappearance of the president during the mutiny is derived from Dr Nyerere and Tanzania. Bobby's and Linda's journey 'south', based in part on a day-long drive Naipaul made between Nairobi in Kenya and Kampala in Uganda (see 1987, p.151), is similarly derived from different East African landscapes, and no place names are offered. As a journey it is literally impossible, as is common in fiction, but here that helps to confirm its symbolic resonance. Few of the characters are named, and in so far as Africans are identified, they are named after places:

Sammy Kisenyi (Bobby's 'minister') after a town in Ruanda, John Mubende-Mbarara (the painter Linda feels has lost his 'primitive' purity) after two towns in Uganda.

5.35   Such parallels with Conrad's earlier narrative are striking. More important, however, is the way in which, while suggesting a closeness of interest, they also indicate the irretrievably post-colonial perspective of Naipaul's text, as it implicitly locates itself in relation to what one might call (adapting Sara Suleri's 'The geography of *A Passage to India*', Reader, p.246) the Western narrative paradigm of Africa. A good example is provided by the account of the army prisoners Bobby and Linda discover towards the end of their journey, in the deposed king's territory:

> They were sitting on the ground; some were prostrate; most were naked. It was their nakedness that had camouflaged them in the sun-and-shade about the shrubs, small trees and lorries. Bright eyes were alive in black flesh; but there was little movement among the prisoners. They were the slender, small-boned, very black people of the king's tribe, a clothed people, builders of roads. But such dignity as they had possessed in freedom had already gone; they were only forest people now, in the hands of their enemies. Some were roped up in the traditional forest way, neck to neck, in groups of three or four, as though for delivery to the slave-merchant. All showed the liver-coloured marks of blood and beatings. One or two looked dead.
>
> (p.228)

ACTIVITY

Now read the following extract from *Heart of Darkness*. This is what Conrad's Marlow finds as he reaches the Company Station, where blasting is in progress. What similarities and differences do you notice between this and the preceding passage?

> A slight clinking behind me made me turn my head. Six black men advanced in a file, toiling up the path. They walked erect and slow, balancing small baskets full of earth on their heads, and the clink kept time with their footsteps ... each had an iron collar on his neck, and all were connected together with a chain ... At last I got under the trees ... Black shapes crouched, lay, sat between the trees, leaning against the trunks, clinging to the earth, half coming out, half effaced within the dim light, in all the attitudes of pain, abandonment, and despair. Another mine on the cliff went off, followed by a slight shudder of the soil beneath my feet. The work! And this was the place where some of the helpers had withdrawn to die ... These moribund shapes were free as air – and nearly as thin. I began to distinguish the gleam of the eyes under the trees ...
>
> (Conrad, *Heart of Darkness*, 1971, pp.16–17)

SAMPLE ANSWER/DISCUSSION

In both these groves of death (as Conrad called his) we are drawn in to witness the anonymous suffering of African people, treated like slaves, swept aside by those more powerful, or simply abandoned. Both passages offer chilling reminders of the human cost of the larger movements of history. But different histories are invoked: Conrad's workers have been discarded by the great 'civilizing', road-building, overseas mission of imperialism, and left to die; Naipaul's prisoners have been captured by the new African government of their country, and are being forced into submission to the post-imperial order. Both narrators draw an ironic resonance from the idea of freedom: for Conrad, the exploited 'were free as air – and nearly as thin'; for Naipaul 'such dignity as they had possessed in freedom had already gone'. The imperialists claimed to be freeing their subjects from enslavement to pagan brutality, but brought their own cruel enslavement; the independence fighters helped to free their people from the yoke of imperialism, but they also opened the way for new enslavement.

Put like this, it seems as if 'In a Free State' suggests an inevitable cycle of corruption, arising out of the darkness within humanity: the forest-dwellers were 'a clothed people, builders of roads' (elsewhere compared to Roman roads, p.226), yet they have been slaves before, and are becoming so again. Conrad's story, we are reminded from time to time, is being told to a group of men in a boat on the Thames, itself once 'one of the dark places of the earth', as when the Romans came to 'civilize' the Britons (pp.5–6). Both narratives are pervaded by this sense of lengthy historical perspective, of empires rising, falling and rising again, although it is the corruption and decay of empire through the exploitation of difference that receives most emphasis. Though the Conrad text is mainly told in the first person, the perspective in the extract is authoritative, neo-omniscient, isn't it? While Naipaul has chosen to narrate this section of his book in the third person, the comments about the king's people sound almost personal, as if they are being made by an individualized narrative voice.

5.36   The question of narrative voice is difficult and subtle here – more so than elsewhere in *In a Free State*. Conrad's account of his 'manner of telling' catches Naipaul's well: it was, Conrad once wrote, 'perfectly devoid of familiarity as between author and reader', yet 'aimed essentially at the intimacy of a personal communication'; and the difficulty we might have with it was because of its 'fluid' and shifting perspective (letter, 14 July 1923, quoted in the Norton edition of *Heart of Darkness*, pp.156–7). And in fact Naipaul himself has testified (quoted in Hamner, 1977, p.54) that Conrad was 'the first modern writer I was introduced to' (by his aspiring-writer father). Conrad's books, especially those set abroad such as *Heart of Darkness* and *Nostromo*, came to provide 'a vision of the world's half-made societies' that answered 'something of the political panic' Naipaul felt as he turned towards those societies for his subject (ibid., p.59). He said:

> Conrad had been everywhere before me ... [He had] meditated on my world, a world I recognize today. I feel this about no other writer of the century. His achievement derives from the honesty which is part of his difficulty, that 'scrupulous fidelity to the truth of my own sensations'.
>
> (quoted in Hamner, 1977, pp.59–60)

5.37   This 'honesty', this 'fidelity' to his own 'sensations', is something Naipaul aims at too. How does it manifest itself in his post-Conradian, post-colonial narrative? In the first place, it's in his drive to undermine the stock response, to show up the hypocrisy that glamorizes or sentimentalizes the situation of people in the newly 'free' states of the world. Nadine Gordimer, another post-colonial anatomist, praised Naipaul's 'In a Free State' on the book's appearance precisely for the accuracy of its exploration of how 'two rather seedy members of the master race' see themselves and their surroundings. In particular, she noted their contempt for the very society that grants them the 'freedoms' they seek – a contempt that, in Bobby's case, is complicated by his 'liberal' views, his conscious struggle to criticize Linda's cruder judgements (Gordimer, 1971, p.5). But in the second place, I'd suggest, Conrad's individualist and ahistorical assumptions have helped shape Naipaul's narrative: although *In a Free State* creates a sense of histories (as in the above extract), that is undermined by the presentation of Africa as an arena for the futile struggles of the decolonized, mimic men (forest-dwellers with 'English' hairstyles) set against a backdrop of irrational, timeless grandeur. This latter point touches on the question of Naipaul's racism, which we will be coming to in a moment.

5.38   But first, it's important to show how – to bring out both points – we need to give close attention to the texture of the narrative. For example, only by doing this can we see how scrupulously Bobby's position – and not just Linda's more obviously questionable views – is undermined by the 'honesty' and even-handedness of the author. This is a matter as much of small shifts of sympathy and perspective from line to line, as it is of the larger, 'set-piece' scenes such as the exchange between Bobby and the Africans at the roadside filling-station (pp.143–9) which you can hear discussed in Radio 12.

ACTIVITY

Consider, for example, this little exchange between the two travellers during an evening walk after dining at the colonel's hotel. The lakeside boulevard is apparently deserted, a shabby reminder of colonial glories:

> 'It's funny,' Linda whispered, 'how you can forget the houses and feel that the lake hasn't even been discovered.'
>
> 'I don't know what you mean by discovered,' Bobby said, not whispering. 'The people here knew about it all the time.'
>
> 'I've heard that one. I just wish they'd managed to let the rest of us know.'
>
> (p.187)

How is Bobby's position shown up, exactly? And what do you feel about Linda's response?

SAMPLE ANSWER/DISCUSSION

Clearly, Linda's response indicates that Bobby's eagerness to display his critical ear for expatriate cliché is itself a stock response. Her whispered comment is innocent in intent, supposed presumably to communicate a sense of awe at the silence, the emptiness of the place, its decayed grandeur, although it is also an example of how expatriate discourse takes over such responses. Bobby's criticism is undermined as he makes it, by that little narratorial insert, 'not whispering', which implies that *he* has no need to hide what he says or thinks about his surroundings. Linda turns this neatly into a joke. And yet, is it a joke we can simply accept? The ideology of imperialism continues to provide the parameters for her humour, doesn't it? The pronouns alone imply as much, the use of 'they' and 'us'. Who are 'they', who are 'us'? As soon as you think about the history that made this colonizers' discourse available, you begin to ask how 'they' could have informed 'us' of their world. And, why should they have?

In short, Bobby is shown to be equally imprisoned within the post-colonial discourse he tries to distance himself from. Furthermore, he needs the black people of this 'free state' to bolster his view of himself as a friend and supporter of their cause, which he serves to the point of betraying white-colonial loyalties – for example, when he informs the new government (itself corrupt) about the South African Denis Marshall's corruption. This is also a personal betrayal, we realize, since it was Marshall who helped his old Oxford chum Bobby to escape persecution and breakdown at home by getting him his present job in Africa. Naipaul's narrative strategy appears to be to allow none of his characters to escape condemnation, usually in the implication of their own remarks, only very occasionally aided by narratorial comment.

5.39 But where, then, *is* the narrator? Is he so very detached, not to be implicated within his own set of discourses? This question is all the more important when we consider how Naipaul himself gets attacked for his racism in this story and elsewhere. 'In a Free State' has drawn particular criticism on this score, for example by Adewale Maja-Pearce, whose extended attack on Naipaul (and his writer-brother Shiva) was prompted by *In a Free State* – or rather, 'In a Free State': he doesn't mention the other stories in the book.

ACTIVITY

Please now read carefully the following extracts from Maja-Pearce's 'The Naipauls on Africa: an African view', which I give at some length because of its importance:

> Nothing is more calculated to infuriate Africans than the arrogance with which foreigners take it upon themselves to pass judgement upon them and their continent ... The Naipaul brothers are merely the latest in a long line of such people. They despise Africans with a passion and they make no secret of it. Take V.S. Naipaul's *In a Free State* ... Africans appear in only very minor roles (not necessarily a criticism) but he leaves us in no doubt of the physical distaste they arouse in him: 'The African opened the door himself. He filled the car with his smell'; 'The boy was big and he moved briskly, creating little turbulences of stink'; 'The tall boy came to clear away Bobby and Linda's plates and left a little of his stink behind' [pp.136; 175; 178]. And not only Africans but Africa itself has a bad smell; in the words of one of the main characters:
>
> > ... I got it this time, when we came back from leave. It lasts about half an hour or so, no more. It is a smell of rotting vegetation and Africans. One is very much like the other.
> >
> > [p.139]
>
> Academics have attempted to excuse this by pointing out that it isn't only Africans who smell bad:
>
> > There is little point in objecting to his emphasis on physical unpleasantness ... words like 'fat' and 'smell' enter the story as part of Linda's vocabulary and are adopted as Naipaul's from the Hunting Lodge incident onwards; but the same points are made about the Colonel ...
> >
> > [White, 1975, p.200]
>
> This is true, but it misses the point: the Colonel is the only European who smells, and he is portrayed as a figure of pity, as a man who, trapped by Africa and his own weakness, has become contaminated ... V.S. Naipaul is equally keen on the ideal of Africa as a place of lies ... the Naipauls' constant quips have become automatic reflexes over which they have lost all control ... everything is reduced to farce ... derision ...
>
> But no one is denying that Africa is in a state of tremendous upheaval; no one is denying that many of the perversions of modern Africa are absurd ... But our laughter [at its tyrants] is tempered by the knowledge of the suffering they cause, suffering which affects real people who feel real pain. The laughter of the Naipaul brothers isn't tempered by this knowledge because, to them, Africans can't be taken seriously: in an insidious way they don't exist for them as real people. This is what offends. And the key to their attitude lies in their worship of the West and the Western tradition ... ironically, as West Indians, they are themselves products of a society struggling to find itself after the bloody legacy of defeat and enslavement at the hands of the very tradition they extol.
>
> (Maja-Pearce, 1985, pp.111–12, 114–16)

Are you persuaded by this argument? If not, how would you counter it, using the text of 'In a Free State'? Look closely at the passages Maja-Pearce cites, and bring in any others you think are relevant.

SAMPLE ANSWER/DISCUSSION

As you may have noticed, this develops the criticisms that Lamming and Sivanandan made about Naipaul (although Maja-Pearce focuses more sharply on racism in the African context). They, too, are uneasy about Naipaul's satiric vision, which they see as a 'wholesale' adoption of the 'Western tradition'. But Maja-Pearce – in an echo of Achebe's attack on 'colonialist critics' (Reader, pp.271–9) – goes a step further, rebutting the 'academics' who defend Naipaul. In my view, the argument is to some extent unanswerable. Naipaul does make many of his African characters distasteful in precisely the offensive, physical manner Maja-Pearce enumerates, while excluding the whites unless they are, and this is significant, crippled in some way, such as the Colonel – or (as Maja-Pearce might have added, but doesn't) *women*: Linda's smell and her pathetic attempt to deodorize it lead to Bobby's appalling outburst, in which he accuses her of being 'nothing but a rotting cunt', along with 'millions more' colonial wives (p.219). It is arguable that this reveals no more than Bobby's obvious and predictable misogyny, and is the product of his sexual disappointment and fear. So, too, you could argue, Linda's remarks about the rotten smell of Africa and Africans are 'placed' by their context: a glance at page 139 shows she is reacting against the ridiculous Marshalls and their exoticizing talk about their beloved 'smell of Africa', even as they decide to clear out and head back to their South African homeland; she is also repeating (while claiming it makes her ashamed to do so) the views of her dubious husband Martin.

But what about Maja-Pearce's point that it is Naipaul who makes the specific comments? I think you will find on close analysis that in each of his examples there is at least a question about who is speaking at that moment in the narrative. Naipaul's frequent and subtle use of free indirect speech suggests that we are inhabiting the expatriate consciousness, and not the narrator's (much less the author's). Does this undermine the overall argument? Not quite, since there is still the question of how adequately the author has distanced himself from the racism of his characters. Further, there are other, sometimes more extended examples of narratorial commentary which can be used to support the general argument, if not the specific one about the text's emphasis on distasteful physical detail.

Did you notice, for example, how the African servants at the colonel's hotel are characterized? Peter, Timothy and Carolus (whom Bobby tries to seduce) are individualized to an extent, but for the rest we only hear – in the repeated phrase – their 'squealing' and 'high-pitched chatter', as if they were not fully human: indeed they are 'like the birds', says the colonel, they are 'Fresh from the bush' (p.184). And if this is defended as part of the story's emphasis on the marginalization of the king's people – the forest people who are, as we've seen, enslaved by the new president's army – there remains the problem of what we make of a people we only see from the outside, and who are depicted as somehow part of nature, exoticized afresh by Naipaul's imagination which, to that extent, seems to share, at least as much as it criticizes, the settler vision exemplified by the colonel.

5.40   This is where Naipaul's narrative appears, on close inspection, to inhabit the same questionable area of discourse as Conrad's, that discourse in which, for example, Conrad makes Marlow talk of the necessity of having to 'put up with sights, with sounds, with smells, too, by Jove! – breathe dead hippo so to speak, and not be contaminated' (*Heart of Darkness*, p.50): in short to contemplate unflinchingly the barbaric practices ('unspeakable rites', he calls them, p.51) revealed by penetration into Africa. It is the abiding aura of mystery, the incomprehensibility, of the forest people as depicted by Naipaul which renders them similarly 'other'. Their chatter is, we're told at the start of the hotel episode, the 'language of the forest', hence its incomprehensibility (p.169). Similarly incomprehensible, but more mysterious and suggestive of the unspeakable, are those running men painted white, who emerge from the 'bush'/'forest' and who, in one Penguin edition, are displayed on the cover, presumably as an invitation to contemplate their exotic nakedness. Naipaul is not responsible for the cover of his book, and the moment of their mysterious emergence is framed by his two expatriate protagonists, so that the way they are described *can* be understood as a continuation of the expatriate viewpoint. But, is it?

ACTIVITY

Re-read pages 210–11, from 'They drove towards the plain' to 'the helicopter ... was no longer to be heard'. What do you make of the metaphors used to describe the men? Whose perspective do you think we're being invited to share?

SAMPLE ANSWER/DISCUSSION

It seems to me that the narrator and his characters are inseparable in their perception of these men, involved as the latter are in some ritual known only to themselves, and as much part of nature ('white as the knotted, scaly lower half of the tall cactus plants', etc.), as alien or 'other', as any colonial imagining of the primitive. This isn't to deny the powerful resonance of the moment, and the inadequacy of Bobby and Linda's perceptions that it suggests. The aim, rather, is to show how Naipaul's imaginative perspective readily accommodates the familiar and dehumanizing stereotyping in Western, if not racist, ideology.

This is the more obvious if you consider for a moment how such a scene would appear in *Things Fall Apart*. Naipaul's narrative isn't as patronizingly limited as the district commissioner's at the conclusion of that novel, although the Maja-Pearce viewpoint would presumably see them as similar. On the other hand, the scene is a long way from inviting our sympathetic understanding for a people whose world has been destroyed, as the forest people's has been. Or are we being unfair on Naipaul? The narrative tone of 'In a Free State' is remarkably neutral, uncommitted, and to that extent is subject to different interpretations.

Exploring 'In a Free State's covert encounter with *Heart of Darkness* highlights one way in which Naipaul's text may be said to *reinforce* the colonialism that it seems to be attacking. But it also suggests the possibility of subverting the residual colonial discourse present in the post-colonial era. And there remains the fact that 'In a Free State' is only one – if very important – part of the whole sequence of narratives, the last of which we haven't yet considered in detail.

Conclusion: 'The Circus at Luxor'

5.41 The ambiguities and contradictions that our scrutiny of Naipaul's title-story have begun to produce are not resolved by the epilogue, in contrast to what we might expect. But they are taken onto a new level of interpretative possibilities. As I've been saying, the book as a whole seems to ask to be read as a layered series of narratives, framed by the prologue and epilogue. Rather than proposing one final or fixed reading of the epilogue, then, it may be more appropriate to put forward at least two clearly differentiated responses, and for you to choose the one you find more persuasive in your re-reading of the book. This has the added advantage of presenting you with the main alternative ways of responding to the book, although, as I shall point out, one of them has tended to predominate.

5.42 Dickens's circus people in *Hard Times* may be said to offer an alternative set of possibilities for a mid-Victorian Britain stubbornly determined upon a path of continuing exploitation and hard-headed profit. In the context of a post-imperial world, what are we to make of the circus people in the concluding section of Naipaul's book? We cannot ignore the fact that it *is* concluding, the deliberately placed last piece of narrative, nor that it obviously echoes the themes and situation of the prologue. Recording a second visit to Egypt, this time from Italy, the journal writer of the prologue finds himself once again surrounded by people of various nationalities, contemplating the remains of empire: the country and its people are still nominally free and, again, the Greeks and Lebanese are discussing how to make money (out of illegal Rhodesian tobacco, ironically enough) while the peasant poor are disregarded as before. Once again, an act of gratuitous violence takes place, and various responses to it are depicted. Exploiter and exploited are involved in an unpleasant 'game', once again focusing on the main themes: freedom, power, order and their lack in the post-colonial dispensation.

ACTIVITY

But what *differences* do you notice between the prologue and epilogue? And what do you make of them? How do they contribute to the concluding effect of the book as a whole?

SAMPLE ANSWER/DISCUSSION

The most obvious difference is that this time, far from just observing what happens when the Italians toss the food at the beggar boys to film them being beaten away by the man with the camel-whip – as would have been consistent with the careful, reluctant and neutral prologue narrator – the journal writer (whom we cannot help taking as the author) intervenes. He takes away the whip, and threatens to 'report this to Cairo' (p.243). It is as if Linda's urge to use a whip has found its analogy, just as the forest-people have become the desert boys who spring up 'like sand-animals' around the institutions of the decolonized state. Naipaul's resistance to sentimentality or hypocrisy continues in the narrator's awareness that, nevertheless, nothing is achieved by his action, and he feels 'exposed, futile' (p.243). But this time it is the narrator, not one of his characters, who thus expresses himself.

Even more notable, however, is the presence of the Chinese, who present medals, postcards and peonies to all the ragged Egyptian waiters:

> Peonies, China! So many empires had come here. Not far from where we were was the colossus on whose shin the Emperor Hadrian had caused to be carved verses in praise of himself, to commemorate his visit. On the other bank, not far from the Winter Palace, was a stone with a rougher Roman inscription marking the southern limit of the Empire, defining an area of retreat. Now another, more remote empire was announcing itself. A medal, a postcard; and all that was asked in return was anger and a sense of injustice.
>
> (pp.245–6)

If US world-power was alluded to in the prologue, here it is the potential world power of the Chinese that is being proposed as taking over the cycle of empires from the distant past. But, unlike the Americans, or any other of the people depicted in the book, the Chinese are presented as a finely made, relaxed, gentle and self-contained people – above all, a community and, what is more, a community of artists.

So: do we take it that the narrator's display of 'anger and a sense of injustice' is what is being asked of us, in the context of the new order in the making? And that his decision to act, which this produced, is to be understood as positive, despite his own immediate reaction to it himself? Or does his feeling of exposure and futility represent more truly the impulse behind this scene, and the book as a whole? For Peggy Nightingale:

> Naipaul thus suggests that the world's peoples are no more than a cosmic circus responding to the crack of fate's whip. Those who imagine themselves to be in a free state are in reality the prisoners of the colonial experience; each is a citizen of a world that offers neither security nor fulfilment. Through several fictional permutations of the basic elements of the post-colonial experience, Naipaul shows that each attempt to relocate leads to misunderstanding and further dislocation. But there is no escape, for all that has occurred is predestined by history and irreversible … With this work of genius, he views the road ahead and discovers only a bleak terminus for humanity's journey.
>
> (Nightingale, 1987, p.171)

John Thieme, on the other hand, argues that, in dropping his earlier masks of irony and anonymity, and coming forward to protest and stop the whipping,

> the act of humanitarian concern has been performed. Though in one sense it is futile (the children jostling for crumbs at the tables of the rich are willing whipping-boys), the gesture of protest nevertheless shows the extent of Naipaul's movement beyond the *karma*-like detachment of the colonial/determinist mentality … Writing on this subject several years ago, I concluded that the sense of 'new found freedom' which Naipaul himself appeared to have found represented 'a very real movement towards a third-world consciousness'.
>
> (Thieme, 1987, pp.161–2)

Thieme first used the phrase 'a very real movement towards a third-world consciousness' in 1975. The appearance of Naipaul's *Guerrillas* in that same year, however, made him 'regret' using it (it does, in any case, require considerable unpacking). Nevertheless Thieme's original view does still represent an arguable position, and one that you should consider – especially since, as is so often the case with a living author, later works are appearing that might make you want to reconsider it.

5.43   What strikes me most in re-reading the book is the last but one paragraph, and the extraordinary, moving note of almost universal despair it sounds: it looks back to 'the only pure time, at the beginning, when the ancient artist, knowing no other land, had learned to look at his own and had seen it as complete'. The longings of the exile in a time of universal upheaval seem to touch him most; but this is perhaps the result of reading into it yet another recent work, *The Enigma of Arrival*, in which the *acceptance* of his incomplete, impure state (a Hindu-Brahmin notion?) provides creative renewal. But what, then, of the *very* last lines, anticipating another cycle of war and defeat, which leaves the Egyptian peasant soldiers 'lost, trying to walk back home, casting long shadows on the sand'?

6 A sense of place: 'The Painter of Signs'

A sense of place

6.1   What do we mean when we talk about a sense of place in a writer's work? Vivid descriptions of scenery, cities or journeys? An awareness that different political and physical geographies shape people's lives in diverse ways? We might mean either. But we might also think of a sense of place in still broader terms – as a cultural identity, a landscape of tradition that can give a writer clarity and purpose. Seen in this way, a sense of place becomes one of the means by which literature defines the continuing part it has to play in a changing world. It follows that a sense of displacement has profound political implications for those writing in a colonial or post-colonial society. Edward Said reminds us of what is at stake: 'For the native, the history of his/her colonial servitude is inaugurated by the loss to an outsider of the local place, whose concrete geographical identity must thereafter be searched for and somehow restored' (Reader, p.36).

6.2   But searching for roots in the lost place will sometimes lead a writer to find something more unsettling than that wished-for 'geographical identity'. The quest for origins, with its uncertain consequences, is a pervasive feature of new writings in English. You have already met ambivalent constructions of place in your work for this block – the vanquished traditional village in Achebe's *Things Fall Apart*, for instance, or the bleak landscapes of V.S. Naipaul's *In a Free State*. If Naipaul's protagonists are looking for a place of their own, the 'free state' that will validate their compromises and defeats, they are bound for disappointment. It might, however, be argued that Naipaul's brooding analyses of disillusionment should not be seen in primarily local terms. If we choose to see his fiction as a philosophical rather than political assertion that no one can ever reach a 'free state', the implications of his work might seem to claim a universality that moves beyond the specific conditions of his own sense of exile as a writer.

6.3   Not everyone will be satisfied with such a reading of Naipaul, and you may well wish to take issue with it yourself. This is a debate that reverberates throughout your work in this block. If we see post-colonial literature as local in its motivation, defined by the cultural and political circumstances that produce it, does this exclude its claim to transcend the conditions of its production? These contending approaches may be pursued through the work of R.K. Narayan, the Indian novelist whose *The Painter of Signs* (1976) we will be studying in this section. Narayan has spent his life in India, the nation that was once seen as the chief glory of the British Empire; the sense of place pervading his writing is in part a response to that cultural situation. Unlike Naipaul, however, Narayan has retained contact with the Hindu culture in which he was brought up. He sees himself as part of a community with religious and cultural roots that run deeper than his situation as a post-colonial writer. He proclaims a confident identity as an Indian writer, while insisting that he has the freedom to write about concerns that are not simply Indian.

6.4   You may recall that, in his introduction to the block, Dennis Walder commented on the strong sense of place in Narayan's work. It's something that Narayan's readers can hardly fail to notice, for one location dominates his books. Throughout a long writing career, Narayan has 'stuck to the setting of an imaginary South Indian Tamil community called Malgudi' (paragraph 1.25). It is a town with very few white inhabitants. Though the evidence of a European presence (the Albert Mission College, the courts, the railway system, the police station ...) is everywhere, this is a town possessed and run wholly by Indians. Malgudi colourfully evokes many of the characteristics of the South Indian cities where Narayan has spent his life – Madras, Mysore, Bangalore. But Narayan reminds us that Malgudi is not to be found in any atlas. It is, he points out, 'my own town', a place that he is free to shape for his own purposes: 'In Malgudi no one can tell me how it should be' (interview, *The Sunday Times*, 23 April 1989). But what happens in Malgudi could – according to Narayan – happen anywhere: '...as he says, small town life is the same everywhere. "That's the thing that appeals to everybody"' (interview, *The Observer*, 18 March 1990). Securely rooted in one place, Narayan wants his fiction to reach out to us all.

Placing Narayan

6.5   How are we to place Narayan? Generation, as well as geography, locates a writer. Narayan was born in 1906. That means he was seventy years old when *The Painter of Signs* appeared. When his first novel, *Swami and Friends*, was published in 1935, India was still very much part of the British Empire. Narayan was a man in his forties, with three novels behind him, when his country achieved independence in 1947. He has lived through far-reaching movements in the cultural and political life of India, and his fiction is formed by the confrontation between Europe and Asia that lies behind this lifetime of change. This confrontation is at the heart of *The Painter of Signs*. But it is treated very differently from – for instance – the devastating clash between Western and African values in Chinua Achebe's *Things Fall Apart*. In order to understand this difference, we need to know something about its origins.

6.6   It's not simply a matter of differing levels of awareness. Narayan, articulate and sophisticated, is constantly alert to the pressures that have shaped the society he writes about. Yet he has never – even in *Waiting for the Mahatma* (1955), in which he deals most directly with the revolutions that have swept through Indian life – chosen to claim an overtly political identity for his work. Born into a Tamil Hindu family, Narayan is able to align himself with traditions that predate the arrival of the British in India by more than a thousand years. Hindu life is rooted in the hierarchical principle of caste, in which people are assigned by birth a fixed position within the structure of the community. The caste system rests on a three-part division of society. The priestly Brahmins represent spiritual power, and are given the highest place. Next come the Kshatriyas, who claim their status as warriors and administrators. The Vaisya are the working mass of the population, earning their living as merchants, farmers and artisans. Excluded from this system altogether are the Indras, or 'untouchables', who are assigned no place within the regulated divisions of caste, and whose lives have generally been characterized by terrifying poverty and deprivation. This ancient social structure has been eroded by countless subdivisions and changes that have evolved over the centuries since its earliest origins. Now unsupported by official sanction – untouchability was outlawed within the Indian constitution in 1950 – the traditions of caste continue to exercise a far-reaching influence over those regions of India where the Hindu religion is dominant.

6.7   Narayan, like Naipaul, was born a Brahmin. This has not blinded him to the situation and sufferings of those less favourably placed, and his writing demonstrates his deep compassion for people condemned to an endless struggle for the simplest means of subsistence. But Narayan's position as a Brahmin has given him access to a forceful source of cultural confidence. He has never lost touch with a past that represents generations of very considerable power and influence. Exile (taking many forms) is as you have seen a prominent feature of the work of many of the writers you have been studying in this block. Narayan is an exception to this pattern. Born in

Madras, a coastal city of South India, he moved as a boy to Mysore, also in South India, which has been his home ever since. His father, as headteacher of the Collegiate High School that Narayan attended, was a figure of importance in both European and Indian terms in the local community. Narayan has now become such a figure himself, a fêted emblem of continuity and success in Indian literary life.

6.8 This sense of a rooted past is not just a matter of the stability of caste or of location. In *My Days*, the volume of his memoirs published in 1974, Narayan recalls his literary inheritance, also rooted in venerable tradition. The Hindu culture of the Tamils has been part of Narayan's experience from his very earliest years. And the Hindus have, as Dennis Walder has reminded you (see paragraph 1.22), a literature of their own. It is old and extensive, and those who are familiar with its countless stories of gods and demons, heroes and mortals, have no reason to feel intimidated by the prestige of Western literary traditions. The story-telling that is an essential part of the Hindu religion transcends the barriers of caste. Nor is it always a matter of printed texts. You don't need to be able to read and write in order to listen and look, and the experience of hearing these stories recited, or seeing them on the cinema screen or even nowadays in the form of comic strips, has been for generations and is still an important part of Hindu life.

6.9 Speaking of one of the oldest Hindu epics, Narayan remarks that 'It may sound hyperbolic, but I am prepared to state that almost every individual among the five hundred million living in India is aware of the story of *The Ramayana* in some measure or other' (quoted in Walsh, 1990, p.8). Such tales are part of the fabric of everyday existence, repeated to children at bedtime, learned by heart, enacted as dance-dramas. But they also exist in the form of books, to which access has been more restricted. Narayan made his comment in the introduction to his own English translation (published in 1973) of a Tamil version of *The Ramayana*, which was originally composed in Sanskrit – the most ancient of India's literary languages, knowledge of which was traditionally confined to the Brahmin caste. Narayan has also translated *The Mahabharata*, another great Hindu epic, and has retold a selection of legends in *Gods, Demons and Others*. His vocation as a Hindu novelist could be seen as an extension of the work of the traditional story-teller, a figure who repeatedly turns up in his fiction – beguiling, reassuring and teaching a crowded audience.

6.10 Does this mean, then, that Narayan's work is simply a matter of handing down ancient wisdom in the form of the modern novel? Not altogether. For his continuing engagement with Indian culture has been tempered by an exposure to Western thought that has led him to view with detachment, or even scepticism, some aspects of his literary inheritance as a Hindu. Narayan's early novel *The Dark Room* (1938), his most sombre work, provides a telling example of this scepticism. *The Dark Room* amounts to a remarkably bitter denunciation of the subjected position of women within Hindu culture. The callously self-centred husband (one of Narayan's very few really abhorrent characters) at the centre of the novel justifies his maltreatment of his wife by the precedent of innumerable Hindu legends:

> Didn't all the ancient epics and Scriptures enjoin upon woman the strictest identification with her husband? He remembered all the heroines of the epics whose one dominant quality was a blind stubborn following of their husbands, like the shadow following the substance.
>
> (*The Dark Room*, 1938, p.141)

Narayan has no intention that his readers should take the old Hindu epics as a simple or consistently reliable guide to human conduct. As he commented in 1971, it is in terms of 'the impact of modern literature' (quoted in paragraph 1.22) that he has now come to understand their significance. And by modern literature Narayan means modern Western literature, as well as the literature of modern India.

6.11   What kind of Western culture, then, has Narayan been exposed to? In *My Days* he recalls the European literature he devoured as a bookish youth in his father's school:

> After Scott I picked up a whole row of Dickens and loved his London and the queer personalities therein. Rider Haggard, Marie Corelli, Molière and Pope and Marlowe, Tolstoy, Thomas Hardy – an indiscriminate jumble; I read everything with the utmost enjoyment.
>
> (*My Days*, 1989, p.61)

What Narayan calls an 'indiscriminate jumble' mixes authors one might expect to encounter in an academic context (Marlowe, Pope) with those more usually dismissed as 'popular' literature. Marie Corelli (1855–1924), for instance (you may remember that Achebe also mentions her as a familiar author), had an immensely successful career as an author of romantic melodramas, but is now remembered – if at all – with derision. But Narayan, relishing whatever came to hand in the school library, had no one to teach him that it was unfashionable to enjoy Corelli's spectacularly racy plots:

> Marie Corelli appealed to me most ... I read about a dozen of her novels, and felt a regret at the end of each book that it was not longer than five hundred pages ... I cut out a portrait of her from *Bookman* and mounted it on my bookshelf.
>
> (Ibid., pp.62–3)

ACTIVITY

Narayan's explorations of contemporary literature were equally enthusiastic. Here's his account of his reading as an adolescent, eagerly investigating what was going on in the world of letters.

From this passage, what can we learn about Narayan's origins as a writer? What kinds of writer was he reading? Do you notice any names we might have expected to find, and are missing?

> My father utilized to the utmost all the library budget and any balance left over from other departments such as sports; the result was that the high-school reading-room had on its table magazines from every part of the world. Week-ends, when foreign mail arrived, were an exciting time. Magazines in brown wrappers were brought home straight from the post office in a mail-bag by a servant. They were opened and heaped up on my father's desk – every magazine from *Little Folks* to *Nineteenth Century and After* and *Cornhill*, published in London was there. My father did not mind our taking away whatever we wanted to read – provided we put them back on his desk without spoiling them, as they had to be placed on the school's reading table on Monday morning. So our week-end reading was full and varied. We could dream over the advertisement pages in the *Boy's Own Paper* or the *Strand Magazine*. Through the *Strand* we made the acquaintance of all English writers: Conan Doyle, Wodehouse, W.W. Jacobs, Arnold Bennett, and every English fiction-writer worth the name. The *Bookman* gave us glimpses of the doings of the literary figures of those days, the scene dominated by Shaw, Wells, and Hardy. I knew precisely what they said or thought of each other, how much they earned in royalties, and what they were working on at any given moment. Obiter dicta, personal tit-bits about the writers and their world, the Chesterton–Belloc alliance against Shaw or someone else, the scintillating literary world of London was absorbing to watch. From our room, leaning on our pillows in obscure Bojjanna Lines of Mysore, we watched the literary personalities strutting about in London. Through *Harper's*, the *Atlantic*, and *American Mercury*, we attained glimpses of the New World and its writers.

The London *Mercury*, with its orange cover and uncut pages, was especially welcome. I viewed J.C. Squire as if he were my neighbour. *John o'London* and *T.P.'s Weekly* afforded us plenty of literary gossip about publishers and writers. *The Spectator, The Times Literary Supplement*, and the Manchester *Guardian* in a thin yellow cover. Twenty-four hours were inadequate for all that one got in hand to read. Slowly, I became familiar with critics who mattered and their judgement. Gradually I began not only to read all the novels in the library but also to acquire through the book reviews a critical sense, so that a certain degree of tempering occurred in my early enthusiasms for some writers – such as Marie Corelli for instance.

(*My Days*, 1989, pp.63–4)

DISCUSSION

One thing that strikes me about Narayan's recollections is their robust sense of self-assurance. Whatever Narayan felt as a boy (and of course these memories are reconstructed from an adult perspective), as a man he is not daunted by the sense that he's confronting a powerful culture to which he is denied access. Far from it: he recalls amusement at the 'strutting' literary figures he encountered as a boy. Narayan exults in the breadth of the reading that his privileged position as headteacher's son opened to him. He remembers the magazines arriving 'from every part of the world'; in practice, though, it seems to have been the publications from London that made the deepest impression. 'Through the *Strand* we made the acquaintance of all English writers: Conan Doyle, Wodehouse, W.W. Jacobs, Arnold Bennett, and every English fiction-writer worth the name.'

All English writers? *Every* English fiction-writer worth the name? What struck you about the literary recollections that Narayan comes up with? Conan Doyle, P.G. Wodehouse, W.W. Jacobs, Arnold Bennett, G.B. Shaw, H.G. Wells, Thomas Hardy, Hilaire Belloc, G.K. Chesterton … it's an impressive list. But one thing you might well have noticed is that these are not (with the exception of Wodehouse) names that have figured prominently or indeed at all on this course. Narayan's reading doesn't seem to have included much poetry (though it was as a poet that Hardy was publishing in Narayan's youth), so it's perhaps not surprising that Yeats, Ezra Pound and T.S. Eliot don't loom large among his memories. And it would have been too early (Narayan is recalling reading in the early 1920s) for him to have discovered Auden – or Graham Greene, later to be a warm friend and supporter. But what about Virginia Woolf? Or E.M. Forster? D.H. Lawrence? James Joyce? Where are they?

Nowhere, as far as the adolescent Narayan was concerned. His earliest literary judgement (he learned, belatedly, to revise his approval of Corelli) was formed by a world largely untouched by, or hostile to, the Modernism that has so influenced our sense of the literary history of the twentieth century. J.C. Squire's periodical, *London Mercury*, was at the centre of a literary establishment (known by its enemies as 'the Squirearchy') that was vehemently opposed to both Modernism ('anarchical cleverness') and the writers of Bloomsbury, including Virginia Woolf and E.M. Forster. Our perspectives on literary history can sometimes give a misleading impression of what was felt to be the literary world that mattered at the time. Thousands were reading *The Strand*, while the *Criterion* (edited by T.S. Eliot), where *The Waste Land* was first published, had a print run of only 800 copies per issue in its palmiest days. Narayan is not describing the literary experience of a benighted outsider. His reading has more in common with that of most British people actively interested in books in the 1920s than we might suppose from what has now become a conventional view of the literary history of the twentieth century, though his perspective on that reading was necessarily different.

Narayan was not wholly isolated from literary innovation: the *Mercury* did publish D.H. Lawrence, and in reading *The Times Literary Supplement* he would have come across the anonymous reviews of Virginia Woolf. He continued to read widely, and in later years he met and appreciated a very wide variety of fiction. E.M. Forster, for instance, became a friend. Nevertheless, as a young man it was in the world of J.C. Squire that Narayan aspired to succeed, and it was to J.C. Squire that he sent his first hopeful literary endeavours.

No wonder, then, that Narayan chose to write in English. Pieces in Tamil, or even Sanskrit, would have had little chance of publication in the *London Mercury*. Narayan has never hesitated about opting for English as his mode of expression. It seemed a perfectly natural choice – and, he has argued, a perfectly Indian one. English has, he points out, been spoken within the Indian subcontinent for centuries. Why shouldn't Indians claim it for their own purposes? Narayan allows the English language to argue its case:

> … I will stay here, whatever may be the rank and status you may assign me – as the first language or the second language or the thousandth. You may banish me from the classrooms, but I can always find other places where I can stay. … I am more Indian than you can ever be. You are probably fifty, sixty, or seventy years of age, but I've actually been in this land for two hundred years.
>
> (1988, p.15)

Yet Narayan has mixed feelings about what English culture, and English literature in particular, has done for the self-esteem of his nation. In *The English Teacher* (1945), published just before Indian independence, the protagonist, Krishna, decides to abandon his career as a teacher of English literature in the Albert Mission College, an institution that as its name suggests is solidly modelled on British educational traditions. Mr Brown, the English headteacher (one of the very few white characters to make an appearance in Narayan's fiction), delivers 'a lecture on the importance of the English language, and the need for preserving its purity' (*The English Teacher*, p.2). Krishna is enraged:

> 'Let us be fair. Ask Mr Brown if he can say in any of the two hundred Indian languages: "The cat chases the rat." He has spent thirty years in India.'
>
> (*The English Teacher*, 1945, p.3)

Krishna realizes his anger is bound up with self-contempt, for he has allowed himself to be bought by an education system empty of meaning:

> I was merely a man who had mugged earlier than they the introduction and notes in the Verity edition of *Lear*, and guided them through the mazes of Elizabethan English. I did not do it out of love for them or for Shakespeare but only out of love for myself. If they paid me the same hundred rupees for stringing beads together or tearing up paper bits every day for a few hours, I would perhaps be doing it with equal fervour.
>
> (Ibid., p.9)

Narayan has been consistent in his vehement repudiation of Western education in India, and in *The English Teacher* he tells us why: 'This education had reduced us to a nation of morons; we were strangers to our own culture and camp followers of another culture, feeding on leavings and garbage' (p.205).

This vigorous denunciation may have a familiar feel to you – after all, Walcott and Achebe, among many others, have said something similar. Like Achebe and Walcott, Narayan is the son of a schoolteacher, and his attitude may in part be seen as a reflection of his personal history. His father – a man of

dominant character – had made his career as a headteacher within precisely
the kind of educational establishment that Narayan condemns so forcefully,
and Narayan's hostility towards the European model for education in India
has much to do with his breaking free from his father's very considerable
patriarchal authority.

It's revealing, from this point of view, to compare his situation with that of
his lifelong supporter, Graham Greene. Very much of Narayan's generation
(born in 1904, Greene is two years older than Narayan), Graham Greene – and
not, after all, J.C. Squire – was the man who first helped Narayan find
publication. Greene's loyal championship has much to do with the furtherance
of Narayan's reputation in the English-speaking world throughout the 1930s,
and since. Graham Greene is also the son of a headteacher. Like Narayan, he
is suspicious of the formal study of literature and, again like Narayan, he has
not been altogether pleased to see educational institutions including his work
as part of their curricula. You may have noted this persistent unwillingness to
be solemnified as an object of scholarly attention as one of the most
interesting points to emerge from Narayan's remarks in TV12 *Born into Two
Cultures: Chinua Achebe and R.K. Narayan*. Narayan and Greene both proclaim
entertainment rather than instruction as the proper end of fiction. This view is
in part a defensive manoeuvre against what they see as the predatory
intentions of pedagogic writing of the kind you are now busily reading. In
their view, academic critics are just the kind of people who can't be trusted
not to tell a novelist 'how it should be'.

This common ground between Greene and Narayan is a reminder that
Narayan's cultural situation is ambivalent. His writing is neither wholly
Indian nor wholly European, but an expression of a fertile interaction between
two traditions. 'The post-colonial text is always a complex and hybridized
formation. It is inadequate to read it either as reconstruction of pure
traditional values or as simply foreign and intrusive' (Ashcroft *et al.*, 1989,
p.110). Malgudi is a more enigmatic place than it might seem on first
acquaintance.

Reading *The Painter of Signs*

ACTIVITY

Turning now to *The Painter of Signs*, please read the opening pages as far as
the break on page 15 ('...ideas bubbled up, lingered a while, burst, and
vanished'). How do you think Narayan situates Raman in terms of the
conflicting Indian and European values that we have been thinking about?

DISCUSSION

Narayan begins his novel with a conflict – comically presented, but central to
the cultural dilemmas that his novel will explore. The professional training
undergone by the lawyer who commissions Raman to paint a new sign-board
has evidently not persuaded him to abandon his traditional beliefs. Raman is
exasperated by the lawyer's determination to settle his business according to
the instructions of an astrologer. He is convinced of the power of reason to
govern human affairs: 'I'm a rationalist, and I don't do anything unless I see
some logic in it' (p.8).

Are we led to sympathize with Raman's frustration when the lawyer insists
on the need for ritual to launch his career auspiciously? Hoarse with reciting

holy verse all through the morning, the lawyer cuts a slightly ridiculous figure. Yet Raman's rationalism seems to rest on no very secure foundation. When challenged, his authority wilts:

> 'All our great minds, from Valluvar down to Bernard Shaw and Einstein, say...'
>
> 'Say what?' asked the lawyer, pausing.
>
> 'I couldn't quote,' Raman said, 'even if I were the author of those sentiments, but I'll copy them down for you some day.'
>
> (p.9)

Despite this discomfiting collapse, Raman is clearly both idealistic and intelligent. Seized by 'a sudden sense of fair play', he promises to replace the lawyer's sand-spattered board. His sense of fair play extends beyond his own transactions, for he is painfully aware of national corruption – 'American milk powder meant for the orphans of India and sold on the black market'; the 'wholesale grain-merchant who cornered all the rationed articles and ran the co-operative stores meant for the poor' (p.14). Perhaps Raman's honest rationalism means that he is more out of tune with his evolving community than the aspiring lawyer: 'He would not recognize it, but Malgudi was changing in 1972.' Would you agree that beside the single-minded ruthlessness of the lawyer and his family, Raman's rather dreamy logic gives him a vulnerable, if engaging, air? Is it a little condescending, too? 'Ultimately he would evolve a scheme for doing without money. While bicycling, his mind attained a certain passivity, and ideas bubbled up, lingered a while, burst, and vanished' (p.15). Perhaps you found yourself reminded of E.M. Forster's characterization of Aziz here. If Raman is to be seen as a representative of the all-conquering civilization of the West – and the passage quoted above makes this a very questionable notion – it's certainly not a role that makes him look very formidable.

ACTIVITY

Now read to the end of the novel's first section on page 42 ('...when he met his friends over coffee at The Boardless'). How does Narayan develop the conflict that he established in the opening pages of the novel?

In thinking about this question, give some attention to the function of the narrative point of view in *The Painter of Signs*. You might like to look at your notes on Audio-cassette 1 Side 2, 'Reading narrative fiction', to help you with this exercise.

DISCUSSION

In considering the function of the narrative point of view, you might at first have thought this a fairly simple matter: isn't this a straightforward example of what used to be called simply an 'omniscient' or 'all-knowing' narrator, informing us of everything that goes on in the character's life, and all the thoughts that pass through his head? If you thought this, you weren't far wrong: the narrative voice does assume a complete knowledge of what happens to Raman. You might have noticed moments in the novel where the reader is invited to share this omniscience, judging Raman's actions from a privileged vantage point. We've already picked out one of those moments: when Raman is at a loss to defend his rationalism before the lawyer's deference to astrology (p.9, see above), the reader is placed in a position of complicity with a narrative voice that knows more than its character. The comedy of the moment arises from the disparity between Raman's aspirations and the imperfect knowledge on which they are based. The narrative voice doesn't have to point this out directly: it emerges from what Raman has to say. The comic moments in the novel often seem to work in this way.

But don't we sometimes – and here we find that the position of the narrator becomes more complicated – discover that this 'all-knowing' perspective moves into the 'first-person' and present tense of 'interior monologue', presenting Raman's thoughts and feelings to us directly? In the terms of the audio-cassette discussion, the omniscient voice may generally be dominant, but the subjective focalization upon Raman merges with it at moments. The two viewpoints seem to me to merge, for instance, in the following extract from page 27. It begins with Raman's voice, as we can tell from line 4 ('Must design and finish that piece of work for the Family Planning, Raman told himself one evening'). The passage continues:

> One thing leads to another. Raman's thoughts went on to the production of food, lands lying fallow, and so forth. He told himself: I am not doing the right thing in carrying on with this sign-board painting. I took it up because I loved calligraphy; loved letters, their shape and stance and shade. But no one cares for it, no one notices these values. Like that bangle-seller and the lawyer and the other, who demand their own style and won't pay otherwise. Compromise, compromise; and now this family planner wants – God knows what – black and white, or white and black, shaded or plain?
>
> (p.27)

Here the narrative voice admits the reader directly, and without irony, into a sympathetic presentation of Raman's thoughts. But his thoughts lead us into a central thematic preoccupation of the novel – compromise and uncertainty. Black and white, or white and black, shaded or plain? Perhaps the omniscient narrator isn't quite as all-knowing as we first supposed.

As we learn more of Raman's way of life, we begin to understand more of its contradictions. Despite his declared contempt for money, he spends much of his time trying to secure payment for work he has done. His attempt to rid himself of sexual preoccupations (interestingly, he condemns his distracting fantasies as unholy rather than irrational) is hardly more successful than his bid to rid his life of money: 'at the back of his mind he regretted that he had hurried away from the river-steps instead of observing the woman fully' (p.16). We soon realize that it is not admiration for Daisy's very much more thoroughgoing rationalism that draws him to her.

Yet Raman's compromises and failures are not presented in a severe light. When he lies, it is to save his aunt the bother of cooking for him. Irritated by her adherence to ancient tradition and religion ('How could the Age of Reason be established if people were like this!'), Raman treats her thoughtlessly but not unkindly. And he takes his reversals in fortune patiently – admiring, for instance, the calligraphy on the scrap of paper that is all he gains for his labour in painting the 'Strictly Cash' sign for the bangle-seller. Raman, we are given to suspect, is more divided in sympathy than he is able to realize. His contempt for a world in which cash is all that counts has as much in common with the fragmented philosophy of the Town Hall Professor (note that Western title: this begowned wise man hardly presents himself as a traditional sadhu) as with the Western logic to which he imagines he has given his allegiance. This reader of Plato, Dickens's *Pickwick Papers*, Gibbon's *Decline and Fall*, and *Kural* ('that tenth-century Tamil classic', p.18) has had a cultural education more indiscriminately mixed than anything Narayan describes in his own schooldays. Raman is no more immune to the attractions of a meditative life than the 'Professor' is to the seductions of cash. The conflicts and divisions of Malgudi are not presented as matters of stark opposition. One view melts into another, and no perspective is wholeheartedly validated by the narrative voice.

Please complete your reading of the novel now, if you haven't already done so.

Narayan and women

6.12   We have already noted that one of Narayan's early novels, *The Dark Room* (1938), takes the position of women within Indian society as its central theme. In *My Days*, Narayan explains why he wanted to write about this issue:

> I was somehow obsessed with a philosophy of Woman as opposed to Man, her constant oppressor. This must have been an early testament of the 'Women's Lib' movement. Man assigned her a secondary place and kept her there with such subtlety and cunning that she herself began to lose all notion of her independence, her individuality, stature, and strength. A wife in an orthodox milieu of Indian society was an ideal victim of such circumstances.
>
> (*My Days*, 1989, p.119)

ACTIVITY

In the light of Daisy's role as social rebel in the novel, how far do you think *The Painter of Signs* is to be read as a development of the theme of women's emancipation after nearly forty years of change in India?

DISCUSSION

Not very far, you might well think. If Daisy represents enlightened modern Indian womanhood, then *The Painter of Signs* could be read as a prophecy of her futility and defeat. Daisy's single-minded strength of purpose might be seen to make her pathetic at best, and at worst ridiculous. She seems incapable of forming close relationships, and her departure at the end of the novel is a flight from the intimacy she admits she fears (p.139) rather than an assertion of strength and independence.

Or is it? Is this how you read the novel? It is a defensible interpretation, but it is not the only one. Daisy's crusade against the ever-continuing expansion of India's population might look foolish in the light of what she is up against: the combined powers of tradition and apathy, coupled with the force of sexual desire, make it seem unlikely that Daisy will have any marked impact on the social problem she has taken on. But the problem itself, and the difficulties of its solution, is real enough. In the 1970s, the issue of birth-control was hotly debated in India, as campaigns urging rural populations to limit their fertility evoked widespread protests, on the grounds that the poor were being compelled – either against their will or without their understanding – to accede to policies that did nothing to alleviate the real causes of their suffering. Daisy's obsession causes her to see birth-control as a kind of panacea for the needy, a solution whose apparently logical simplicity ignores the intransigent complexity of social inequalities in India.

Nevertheless, there are moments when the scale of the problem she confronts and her motives in doing so are acknowledged and respected. What, for instance, did you make of her encounter with the pregnant village woman and her husband as she and Raman travel and campaign throughout the countryside? Would you accept that this is a moment where Daisy is sympathetically presented?

> Daisy remained inside the hut for some time, conversing in a low voice, came out, and said to the villager, 'Ten childbirths in twelve years of married life: don't you see that it will kill your wife?
>
> 'True. She is very sickly,' admitted the man. 'I have to spend so much on medicines for her, but nothing helps.'
>
> 'And the children?' she inquired.
>
> 'Six died,' he added sorrowfully. 'God gives and he takes away ... and that's why I thought at least now...'
>
> (pp.50–51)

Here Daisy's work is seen in a distinctly positive light. Compared with the plight of the village woman, Raman's sceptical objections suddenly look trivial.

Is Daisy inspired, then, by a logical altruism that serves to oppose Raman's muddle-headed infatuation within the structure of the novel? Not altogether. As we learn more about Daisy's past, it becomes clear that her actions are as much the result of her personal history as of disinterested rationality. Her sense of oppression in the overcrowded house in which she was brought up, together with her rebellion – sympathetically presented – against the role of a docile Indian wife, is enough to account for the vehemence of her reaction against the traditionally sanctioned role of child-bearing for women. It's worth remembering that Daisy's passion for birth-control is in fact just as ardent as Raman's passion for Daisy: 'within she seemed to carry a furnace of conviction' (p.47). Daisy, like Raman, is motivated by emotion rather than reason.

6.13   In *The Dark Room*, Narayan reserves his deepest compassion for the plight of the Indian wife. But there are, with briefly sketched exceptions like the wretched village woman and the silent teacher's wife, no married women in *The Painter of Signs*. Daisy refuses marriage. And the other woman who plays an important part in the novel is also without a husband: she is a widow. For Daisy, we should recall, is not the only woman in Raman's life. There is also his aunt.

6.14   On first acquaintance, Aunt looks like a simple embodiment of the oppression endured for centuries by Indian women. And so, in a sense, she is. Her life is devoted to the care of the orphaned Raman, and she seems to have few needs or wishes of her own. She is illiterate – though not, given her devoted listening to the religious discourses of the temple, uneducated. And she has, as she reminds her nephew, a story to tell. Raman begins to transcribe it (pp.18–20), but only reaches the point where the death of her husband 'left her barren and widowed'. Nothing more, it seems, is to be added to a life that seems complete in its service of religion and of her nephew.

ACTIVITY

I want now to turn to Raman's aunt's positioning within the structure of the novel. Is she to be seen as the antithesis of Daisy – as self-abnegating as Daisy is self-assertive, as devoted to tradition as Daisy is to change? Or do they reflect each other, having more in common than might at first be apparent? Make notes about the relation between Daisy and Raman's aunt, indicating where you feel they represent opposing points of view, and where they seem to you comparable.

DISCUSSION

One point of comparison that immediately strikes me is that both Daisy and Raman's aunt are exceptionally strong-minded. Both are committed to a particular view of life with a solidity of conviction that makes the men in the novel, and particularly Raman, look limp and wavering. And though both are fond of Raman, neither is prepared to be swayed by his arguments, still less to allow him to divert them from their chosen courses.

But the perceptions of life with which they have identified themselves seem to have little in common. Aunt, the daughter of a Brahmin priest, is a devout and orthodox Hindu. Daisy seems to have shed every vestige of the traditional beliefs of her family. She has adopted a Western name (though not, interestingly, a Christian one, despite the influence of the 'missionary gentleman', p.51), and she lives with a sturdy contempt for conventional opinion, which horrifies Raman's aunt.

It had seemed that Aunt would devote the rest of her days to her nephew's well-being. But she makes another choice. When it looks as though Raman will marry a rootless girl who seems a repudiation of all that she lives by ('*That* girl! What is her caste? Who is she?', p.115), she leaves the house in Ellaman Street to undertake a journey to Benares, where she will end her life in the most auspicious way possible. 'I may live for ten days or ten years or twenty, it is immaterial how long one lives after this stage. It is the ambition of everyone of my generation to conclude this existence at Kasi, to be finally dissolved in the Ganges' (p.119). The departure of Raman's aunt conforms to an ancient Indian tradition, that of removing oneself from home and family in order to find spiritual fulfilment and to allow the lives of others to continue in peace. Narayan has written about this pattern of Hindu life repeatedly, and it becomes the central theme of one of the novels that has become best known in the West, *The Vendor of Sweets* (1967). But it is generally his male characters who opt for such a path. Raman's aunt is unusual, in Narayan's terms, in taking this route as a woman. In her conformity to an ancient Hindu pattern of holiness, Raman's aunt shows herself to be as unlike Daisy as she could possibly be.

Or does she? We've already noticed that Daisy's apparently comprehensive rationalism is belied by the strong emotions that motivate her actions. Could something similar be said of Raman's aunt? It's clear that her choice is rooted in a genuine spirit of devotion, and this, like Daisy's devotion to the cause of birth-control, is respected within the novel. But isn't it also clear that Aunt's behaviour, like Daisy's, is partly prompted by a very personal emotion – her pain that Raman rejects the values to which she has devoted her life? And there are, it seems to me, other points of comparison between Daisy and Aunt. Unworldly, thoughtless of her own comfort, Daisy finally makes a decision to leave Raman that could be seen as the counterpart of the departure of Raman's aunt on her pilgrimage. Daisy, like Raman's aunt, has no time for the Western idealization of romantic love.

> '"I love you", "I like you", are words which can hardly be real. You have learnt them from novels and Hollywood films perhaps. When a man says "I love you" and the woman repeats "I love you" – it sounds mechanical and unconvincing. Perhaps credible in Western society, but sounds silly in ours.'
> (p.98)

And she too despises the materialism that seems an essential part of Western culture. Like Raman's aunt, Daisy is not interested in the acquisition of wealth and security:

A home, in Daisy's view, was only a retreat from sun and rain, and for sleeping, washing, and depositing one's trunk. Her possessions were limited to this ideal – in some ways, very much like Aunt. If Aunt's worldly possessions could go into a little jute bag, Daisy's filled a small tin trunk and a BOAC air-travel bag which the missionary had given her before leaving for the Congo.

(p.130)

For all the cultural gulfs that separate them, much unites the two firm-minded, disciplined, hard-working and ascetic women who dominate the pages of this novel. They could hardly be more different from the defeated wife whose unhappiness haunts *The Dark Room*.

Narayan's India: *The Painter of Signs*, V.S. Naipaul and Graham Greene

6.15 One thing that has emerged from our reading of *The Painter of Signs* is that Narayan's India is by no means as simple as it might look. It's built out of complications and uncertainties, even contradictions. But can we be more specific than that? What kind of India does Narayan offer us in *The Painter of Signs*? And how does the novel present its images of India? One way of thinking further about these questions is to look at responses that other writers have given to Narayan's work.

6.16 You may remember from Section 1 that V.S. Naipaul argues that Narayan gives us an India that is simply incomplete. According to Naipaul, Narayan 'tells an Indian truth. Too much that is overwhelming has been left out; too much has been taken for granted' (1968; quoted in paragraph 1.23). What, then, has Narayan left out of his fictional representation of India? And what has he taken for granted?

6.17 If we judge from Naipaul's own perceptions of life in India – he has written repeatedly about his experiences of the country – we might want to say that Narayan has left out everything that is too disturbing, too unpleasant. Only very briefly, or tangentially, does Narayan confront the scale of the misery and dirt, the squalor that Naipaul unflinchingly reports as the consequences of the desperate poverty that grips much of the nation. More particularly, in Naipaul's view Narayan avoids recording the degradation of the people who are caught up in India's cycles of deprivation. In spite of their self-deceptions, muddles, compromises and defeats, the characters of Narayan's fiction are almost without exception seen as people the reader is able to like and respect. They may be given to thoughtlessness and folly, but they are not brutal, they are not corrupt, and they are not cruel. Narayan's writing exhibits none of the sour anger and contempt that characterizes so much of what Naipaul has had to say about the Third World.

ACTIVITY

The first of the following two passages, describing the accident that causes Raman and Daisy to spend the night together, will be familiar to you from *The Painter of Signs*. The second comes from Naipaul's *India: a wounded civilization*, where he draws a range of dour conclusions as a result of an investigative journey through India. It was published in 1977, the year after the story of Raman and Daisy appeared.

What do these passages have to contribute to our understanding of the ways in which Narayan and Naipaul see the people of India? Do they seem to you to substantiate Naipaul's criticism of Narayan's viewpoint?

It was seven o'clock. They were planning to catch the town bus leaving Koppal at eight for Malgudi. They had been journeying for over three hours now. The cartman suddenly pulled up crying. 'Damned, accursed thing.' The bullock had stumbled and hurt its leg. The cartman got off his seat and went up to examine the injury. The passengers also got down. The old man looked both forlorn and angry. He hit the animal on its haunches with the handle of the whip, and said, 'I knew it'd do this sort of thing.'

'What has happened?' they asked anxiously.

'He has hurt himself – the fool didn't use his eyes, and has injured his leg. Should not a sensible animal use his eyes and see what's ahead, if a pit or furrow is there? The son-of-a...' He made allusions to the mixed-up, ill-begotten progenitors of this creature. He quickly unyoked the animal, took its foreleg in his hand, and examined it with tender care – for all the foul references in his speech. He was almost in tears as he said, 'He can't pull any more.' He stood brooding for a moment as to what he should do.

Daisy and Raman looked rather worried. 'So what do we do?' they asked in unison.

'I'll take him to the village over there, where he will have an application of medicinal leaves...'

To Raman the cartman seemed more preoccupied with the animal's leg than with their fate. He went on elaborating about the medicament for the animal until Raman was forced to inquire, 'What are we to do?'

(*The Painter of Signs*, pp.70–71)

The poor are almost fashionable. And this idea of intermediate technology has become an aspect of that fashion. The cult in India centres on the bullock cart. The bullock cart is not to be eliminated; after three thousand or more backward years Indian intermediate technology will improve the bullock cart. 'Do you know,' someone said to me in Delhi, 'that the investment in bullock carts is equivalent to the total investment in the railways?' I had always had my doubts about bullock carts; but I didn't know till then that they were not cheap, were really quite expensive, more expensive than many second-hand cars in Britain, and that only richer peasants could afford them. It seemed to me a great waste, the kind of waste that poverty perpetuates. But I was glad I didn't speak, because the man who was giving me these statistics went on: 'Now. If we could improve the performance of the bullock cart by ten per cent...'

What did it mean, improving the performance by ten per cent? Greater speed, bigger loads? Were there bigger loads to carry? These were not the questions to ask, though. Intermediate technology had decided that the bullock cart was to be improved. Metal axles, bearings, rubber tyres? But wouldn't that make the carts even more expensive? Wouldn't it take generations, and a lot of money, to introduce these improvements? And, having got so far, mightn't it be better to go just a little further and introduce some harmless little engine? Shouldn't intermediate technology be concentrating on that harmless little engine capable of the short journeys bullock carts usually make?

...

The bullock cart is to be improved by high science. The caravans will plod idyllically to market, and the peasant, curled up on his honest load, will sleep away the night, a man matching his rhythm to that of nature, a man in partnership with his animals. But that same peasant, awake, will goad his bullock in the immemorial way, by pushing a stick up its anus. It is an unregarded but necessary part of the idyll, one of the obscene sights of the Indian road: the hideous cruelty of pre-industrial life, cruelty constant and casual, and easily extended from beast to man.

(Naipaul, 1979, pp.119–24)

DISCUSSION

There is a sense in which I'm asking you to make an incongruous comparison, looking at an incident from a novel next to an extract from a discursive work of non-fiction. Nevertheless, some telling points emerge from the juxtaposition. Narayan's cartman does behave with verbal and physical violence when the bullock hurt his leg. This dismay might well be interpreted as having nothing more than economic causes. After all, the cart is his means of livelihood. Nevertheless, the reader is clearly meant to perceive real concern for the welfare of the bullock behind the cartman's apparent ferocity. He examines the bullock's injury 'with tender care', and is 'almost in tears' when he pronounces him unfit to pull.

Naipaul's peasant seems to come from a different world. The very fact that he is termed a 'peasant' – a word that in English carries inevitable associations of debasement – marks the contrast. Naipaul sees little scope for humanity within the traditional occupation of driving a bullock cart. For Narayan, the association between human and animal suggests the potential for responsibility and affection. But Naipaul perceives it as an expression of what amounts to a bestial way of life, a tradition that allows scant distinction between beast and man. Seen in these terms, the prospect of the hypothetical 'harmless little engine' suggests a positive advancement. It represents progress of a kind that will take India out of a hopeless and stagnant past, the 'waste that poverty perpetuates'.

6.18 Naipaul is sharply suspicious of the reverence for traditional values and activities that he encounters everywhere in India. He sees spirituality as India's heritage, but he interprets it as an exhausted and paralysing legacy. It is in the activities of the mind, rather than the spirit, that Naipaul chooses to place his confidence. Naipaul believes that only progressive reason can help India:

> While India tries to go back to an idea of its past, it will not possess that past or be enriched by it. The past can now be possessed only by inquiry and scholarship, by intellectual rather than spiritual discipline. The past has to be seen to be dead; or the past will kill.
>
> (Naipaul, 1979, p.174)

Here are the deepest grounds of the disagreement between Narayan and Naipaul. '"India will go on"', Naipaul quotes Narayan as saying in 1961 (ibid., p.18). For Naipaul this is a baleful prophecy – catastrophic if it means that India will simply perpetuate a past that needs to be opened to challenge and debate. If the past must be known, it is because it must be overturned.

6.19 But Narayan understands things quite differently. It isn't that he sees Malgudi – or India – as immune to change. New developments, and new problems, present themselves and must be considered. We have seen that *The Painter of Signs* is not hostile to the modernity that Daisy represents. Her rejection of the traditional role of the Hindu wife, and her advocation of the cause of birth-control, are sympathetically treated. But the argument of the novel suggests that Daisy's brand of apparently rational activism is doomed to be limited in effect because it disregards an essential part of human experience. Naipaul asserts that Narayan leaves out 'too much that is overwhelming'. Narayan's answer, as expressed in *The Painter of Signs*, is that Naipaul's ruthlessly intellectual perspective is open to the same charge.

6.20 What, then, does this novel suggest that Naipaul's argument omits? Raman and Daisy are both, in different ways, determined to propel their world into the 'Age of Reason', an ambition of which Naipaul would have approved. Both fail. The central reason for their failure is seen to be their lack of self-knowledge. Their shared impatience with the past has a great deal to do with this deficiency. Did you notice that both have lost their parents, their closest link with their own history? Daisy, quite as bent on shaking off the past as Naipaul could have wished, has rejected her family deliberately and completely in her rebellion against the traditional role of feminine subservience. And Raman, despite the loyal devotion of his aunt, remains an orphan: his parents have been killed, and he is, in terms of the extended Hindu families that usually crowd through the pages of Narayan's fiction, a curiously lonely figure. He is simply irritated by his aunt's efforts to connect him with his past through her repeated anecdotes of family history. Once he has in effect rejected his aunt through his decision to marry Daisy, Raman is entirely isolated within his community.

6.21   Raman and Daisy persistently underestimate the profound influence of the emotions on all human behaviour, including their own. Perhaps the clearest indication of the perceived limitations of their outlook within the novel comes in their encounter with the aged yogi in the cave-temple. Dedicated to the fertility that Daisy opposes, this faintly sinister hermit is clearly no saint. He is by no means impervious to his own interests, and a good deal of his hostility to the visiting pair arises from the fact that Daisy's teaching threatens his status and subsistence. Nevertheless, he represents a kind of power to which Raman and Daisy have no access. He is able (here, as often in his fiction, Narayan introduces a suggestion of the supernatural) to see the past to which Daisy has chosen to close her eyes: 'I'll tell you your past' (p.58). She finds this feat disconcerting: 'Daisy looked somewhat shaken…' (pp.58–9). Raman reacts similarly when he follows the hermit into his temple, characteristically torn between belief and scepticism: 'There was something in this temple which cowed one and made one prattle' (p.63). When modern rationalism and ancient religion meet head on, as they do here, Narayan permits the world of faith a qualified triumph. Little wonder that Naipaul is so scathing about Narayan's fiction.

6.22   It might seem odd that Narayan's most long-standing and celebrated supporter, Graham Greene, comes from the Christian West – rather than from the Hindu background that Narayan shares, from a very different perspective, with Naipaul. But when we consider the relation between Narayan's position and Greene's own fiction, their enduring alliance may seem less strange. Narayan's *The World of Nagaraj* (1990) carries, like so many of his previous books, a cordial recommendation from Graham Greene on its dust-jacket: 'Narayan wakes in me a spring of gratitude, for he has offered me a second home. Without him I could never have known what it is like to be Indian.' Does Narayan show us what it is like to be Indian?

6.23   If so, he does it in a way that might well seem consciously adapted to Western expectations. Like Achebe, Narayan constructs a world in which what is foreign and strange to us is revealed as the everyday business of other lives. He writes about humdrum details – his characters' meals, their clothes, their washing arrangements and domestic pastimes – with an exactitude that gives his fiction, to Western readers, some of the engaging qualities of travel writing, a genre that has always been attractive to Greene. Narayan reminds us of our own place, suggesting that what we take for granted as the fixtures and fittings of European life do not amount to the only possible cultural norm. They might seem strange and exotic, and difficult to interpret, to others. Raman defends Daisy's Western name to his aunt:

> 'Nothing more than the name of a flower, that's all. Daisy is a flower.' He realized that he was not sure what flower it was. 'It's a most lovely flower grown in America, England, and so forth.'
>
> (p.115)

It's intriguing to compare Raman's vagueness here with Naipaul's reflection, in an essay of 1964, that what he had taken to be an equally unknown bloom is in fact a flower he has known all his life: 'Jasmine! So I had known it all those years. To me it had been a word in a book, a word to play with, something removed from the dull vegetation I knew' (1976, p.31). A word, the name of a simple flower, is sufficient to indicate a huge cultural gulf. Greene's own fiction often achieves its effects through the telling use of apparently trivial detail, and Narayan's ceaseless attention to the peripheral particulars of the life of his characters is one of the things that draws the two novelists together.

6.24   Both Greene and Narayan are concerned with the mundane realities of day-to-day living; both write about the economic realities that underpin our existence. Both are interested in the ways in which people make their living. Narayan's novels often bear the names of their protagonist's professions – *The English Teacher*, *The Financial Expert*, *The Guide*, *The Vendor of Sweets*, *The Painter of Signs*. Greene has sometimes chosen similar titles for his novels – *The Confidential Agent*, *The Honorary Consul*. But they might also be seen to share other and perhaps deeper preoccupations which have contributed to a bond which has persisted over the decades.

ACTIVITY

Think back over your reading of Graham Greene's *England Made Me* in Block 3. Do you see any points of comparison that might usefully be made between this novel and *The Painter of Signs*? Are the plots in any way comparable? Do they have similar themes?

DISCUSSION

There are, I think, a number of interesting echoes in terms of the construction of the plot. *England Made Me*, like *The Painter of Signs*, turns on a loving relationship between a man and a woman which finally fails through lack of self-knowledge, and an inability to confront disruptive emotions. In Greene's novel, too, this failure seems to arise out of alienation from a painful past. But Kate and Anthony, still more rootless than Daisy and Raman, live in a more vicious world, and Anthony is finally destroyed through violence of a kind that is never allowed to surface within Narayan's more secure community.

Did you notice any other similarities? I would argue that the most significant is that both books challenge the rational. Greene and Narayan are both dealing with people who have become detached from the spiritual resources of their culture, resources represented by two characters (Minty and the yogi) who have become distinctly down at heel, even seedy, but who nevertheless maintain contact with sources of vitality that are denied to the central characters.

Neither novel achieves anything approaching a happy ending. Greene's novel, as Roger Day reminds us, has some of the vivid action of a thriller, while Narayan's is often comic; nevertheless, both are pervasively melancholic. Human affection is not enough to save Kate, Raman or Daisy from the life of isolation to which they seem doomed at the end of their narratives. Narayan and Greene write from a religious perspective in what they see as a predominantly secular world. They are persistently concerned with alienation, withdrawal and loss. Narayan put it bleakly in *The English Teacher*: 'Wife, child, brothers, parents, friends … We come together only to go apart again … They move away from us as we move away from them … A profound unmitigated loneliness is the only truth of life' (*The English Teacher*, p.203). Here Narayan is writing as a Hindu, and we should recall that the last withdrawal of Raman's aunt in *The Painter of Signs* is not seen as an act of defeat. But what he says might also serve as an epigraph for Greene's joyless stories of spiritual solitude in the West.

6.25   Why conclude this section on a contemporary Indian writer by reminding you of associations between *The Painter of Signs* and a novel published in 1935 by an English writer? My aim is to reinforce the point with which Dennis Walder began the block. Like all the writings you have studied in this part of the course, Narayan's fiction is not simply a 'foreign' body of work, though it is shaped by cultural assumptions and experiences that are very different from those of the West. From the viewpoint of a South Indian Hindu, Narayan engages with controversies and debates that matter to us all. He inhabits a world of which Europe, and European culture, is a part, just as his culture is a part of Europe. It is up to us not to lose sight of that fact. If we do, the loss will be ours.

7   Conclusion: where do we go from here?

7.1   The most important point about the 'new writings in English' is that they call into question the traditional canon of English literature. Though largely ignored or marginalized, their demonstrable interest and quality challenge conventional ways of thinking about ourselves and the world. If, as E.P. Thompson has suggested, there is a sense in which Britain is 'the last colony', reading the new writings may help us to decolonize ourselves – no easy task, as Naipaul's fictional vision of the post-colonial 'free states' of the world makes us realize. But his is only one of many versions of a complex historical process. That should be clear even from the small number of texts we've chosen to explore – from such hugely disparate places as Nigeria (including the different traditions of the Igbo and Yoruba), St Lucia, Trinidad, India and the UK itself. Yet, despite their many differences, all the texts, all the writers studied in this block, have this in common: they all use the English language – even if, as Chinua Achebe long ago remarked, 'we intend to do unheard of things with it' ('Colonialist criticism', Reader, p.274).

7.2   Of course, it is part of the creative, originating force of these writings that they do 'unheard of' things, not only with the language but also with the artistic forms and traditions of the European culture that has held their societies within its grip for so long – and that retains a certain hegemonic control even though its world power has waned. (This shift in power is not simply a matter of 'influence' replacing direct control; rather it has to do with a complex range of interactions, affecting the social, political, economic and cultural relationships between countries, peoples and races worldwide.) If we can respond to the creativity of these new writings, can grasp their main themes and issues, we can develop an awareness of how to respond to and evaluate them for ourselves. If we have done this, it will also make accessible many other texts and writers beyond the bounds of the broadly 'Western' tradition – some of them mentioned in the preceding discussions, in the Reader extracts, or in the accompanying broadcasts.

7.3 'Western' – like the aesthetics, the cultural parameters, which it subsumes – is itself a word you will probably be questioning. Analysing our own discourse is no easy job. But at least we should try to make ourselves aware of how it operates – particularly, as Edward Said has demonstrated in 'The discourse of the Orient' (which you'll already know from Block 5), of how it constructs the world outside the European metropolitan centres as irreducibly different and inferior, as 'other'. Said's agenda, like that of many critics of imperialism such as Frantz Fanon, owes a good deal to the cultural theory of Antonio Gramsci (1891–1937), himself an outsider from a despised and dominated region, imprisoned for his subversive questioning of the grand ambitions of a major European power – Italy (he was a Sardinian). According to Gramsci,

> Obviously East and West are arbitrary and conventional, that is historical, constructions, since outside of real history every point on the earth is East and West at the same time. This can be seen more clearly from the fact that these terms have crystallised not from the point of view of hypothetic melancholic man in general but from the point of view of the European cultured classes who, as a result of their world-wide hegemony, have caused them to be accepted everywhere.
>
> (Gramsci, 1986, p.447)

7.4 Said demonstrates that the cultural manifestations of imperialism – including the self-defining 'literary' – have helped to bolster continuing domination by the 'West'. And even more important, he has suggested how the 'East' has accepted, even collaborated with (consciously or unconsciously), the takeover of its signifying systems. A sense of this (apparently inescapable) trap lies behind the frustration and anger of critics such as Fanon, who focus particularly on the lasting self-contempt that colonialism engenders in black people.

7.5 While these perceptions, and the analysis they produce within literary criticism, can help us grapple with the questions of ideology and history which any serious study of the new writings involves, there remains a gap in this discourse – *gender*. As Jane Miller has pointed out, while Said and Fanon and those who follow in their footsteps use female imagery in their critique of colonialism and imperialist hegemony, women as people are markedly absent from their work. She fully acknowledges the original and interpretive force of their critique, but deplores the absence of connection with feminist theory – especially in Said, who is of course contemporary, and who may therefore be said to be more culpable for seeming to ignore or sidestep what has become an influential mode of thought and politics since Fanon's death. Miller argues:

> Women figure in Said's analysis in a number of ways, but he appears not to see that their presumed sexual availability is itself produced by the transformation already performed on it and on the countries which it then comes to represent. Women and colonies and invaded territories generally become available *because* they are undeveloped, uncultivated, swathed in their natural vulnerability and therefore weak, passive, receptive and intuitive. Their value to the coloniser is for their natural resources. They are likely to be blessed with a crude and unadulterated beauty, which is likely, in its turn, to be marred by a certain coarseness and by an inability to appreciate the finer gifts of their rescuing conquerors. A prevailing imagery of penetration, of stamina and of the eventual discovery of the strange and the hidden at the end of a journey requiring courage and cunning serves to merge the colonising adventure definitively with the sexual adventure.
>
> (Miller, 1990, pp.116–17)

To give Said his due, she continues, there is no doubt that he sets out

> with care and delicacy the parallels and analogies developed in this field between colonial relations and sexual relations, and he shows how

illuminating of the reality of the imperial adventure these parallels have been for both East and West. What he does not confront are the sexual meanings on which those illuminating parallels depend. It is possible to feel that within his analysis it is with the distortions of male sexuality produced by the language of Orientalism that he is chiefly concerned. To undermine the economy, the sovereignty and the culture of another people is, above all, to undermine the identity and integrity of its male citizens. That has often involved the theft of their women, as part of a process which is to be thought of as infantilisation or, ultimately, as feminisation. The question remains: why does such an analysis not entail a concern for women's loss of political and economic status, in itself? The possibility that women had little or no political or economic status to lose does not become part of the history which is being written.

(Ibid., p.118)

What Miller helps to demonstrate is how far the criticism by cultural theorists has transformed our understanding of the interaction between cultures, and our appreciation of both the difficulties and the pleasures to be discovered in approaching other cultures.

7.6   The point is, we want to leave you with the materials to reconsider, or develop, the work you have done elsewhere in the course (such as in Blocks 4 and 5) in the light of what you *now* know about some of the new writings. In this block we have done no more than touch on the gender aspect of the new writings, for instance in Section 4 where you are referred to Elaine Fido's feminist reading of Derek Walcott in the Reader, in Section 5 where you are asked to consider the criticism of Naipaul's sexist handling of Santosh's *hubshi* wife and the characterization of Linda in *In a Free State*, and of course in Section 6 (pp.109ff.). You are about to come onto the whole question of gender and language in the *next* block – where, for example, you will be reading Toni Morrison's *Song of Solomon*. This work was created out of a woman's vision of the unique character of black US history, an experience that has been largely ignored or inadequately narrated by the writers and historians of the dominant white culture, and that Morrison renders visible – indeed, celebrates. The richness of her achievement speaks more powerfully of what might be considered missing from our own chosen texts, or from the criticism of them, than perhaps anything we could now offer. None the less, it may be useful to suggest some starting-points for a feminist reading of new writings.

7.7   For instance, you might like to consider some comments made by my colleague Cicely Havely, on *Things Fall Apart*:

Achebe's narrative is marked by a serene even-handedness: the women have their powers, their responsibilities and their own stories. He extends the same impartial moral equanimity even to the colonial intruders whose arrival heralds the break-up of traditional values. Yet his work has contributed to what Molara Ogundipe-Leslie has called 'the mythification of the rural woman'. Ogundipe-Leslie goes on to suggest that

it seems that the African male needs this myth to buoy-up his conservatism and his yearning for that pre-colonial patriarchal past where he was definitely king as father, husband and ruler. The myth of the unchanging, naïve rural woman seems to coincide with the actual social practice and tendency of men to discourage change and innovation in women's lives.

(Ogundipe-Leslie, 1987)

Achebe's narrative claims to be authentic. Its women live without protest within the hierarchical orders of the tribe. But more recently, African feminists have begun to suggest that such depictions of docile and dignified conformity are in fact mythical, and that it was the patriarchal colonizers who imparted a standard of female subservience which male African writers have opportunistically transferred to their own romantic visions of the pre-colonial past. Katherine Frank (1987) says that 'there is endless debate among writers, critics, journalists, sociologists and anthropologists about whether this entrenched patriarchal culture came with the white colonialists or is inherent in African society'. Perhaps, then, Achebe's orderly society is not so much a historical reality as historical fiction, written out of a masculine nostalgia for that mythical time when a woman knew her place and was happy with it?

7.8   This is an interesting and important question, suggesting how a striking new issue such as the 'mythification' of history is raised by further consideration of one of our texts. Pamela Morris, one of A319's two assessors, in response to an earlier draft of Section 2 of this block on the same novel, argued that gender was registered in a different and more detailed way by Achebe's text:

> I wish you had elaborated more the brief references you make to an opposition in the text between a 'masculine' ethos and a 'feminine' one, both potentially available to the society [of the novel]. Okonkwo kills Ikemefuna because 'he was afraid of being thought weak' – not manly. I don't think in the least the narrative implies this to be accepted as part of the communal rules. In this most carefully structured of stories, Okonkwo's 'recovery' from the killing is signalled by his joke about the disorderly tribes in which 'a man's children belong to his wife and her family' – a reversal of 'natural' order, almost!
>
> This is immediately followed by the narrative of the life-threatening illness of Ezinma, the only child – and a *daughter* – of Okonkwo's first wife, Ekwefi, who married him when he was yet poor. For a whole night Ekwefi refuses to desert Ezinma, defying the might of Agbala and her priestess: she is afraid, but unlike Okonkwo, 'she swore within her that if she heard Ezinma cry she would rush into the cave to defend her against all the gods in the world. She would die with her' (p.76). Ezinma is of course the daughter of whom Okonkwo thinks 'She should have been a boy' (p.44), in contrast to Nwoye whom he despises as effeminate like Okonkwo's father. Nwoye prefers the women's stories of cunning and survival, to those of his father, which glorify death. If this (and *much* more in the text) is not an undermining of the tragic gender rigidity perceived as the fatal flaw in the dominant culture of the tribe, then I don't know what it is!

What do you think? There is, as Pamela Morris so forcibly points out, '*much more in the text*'.

8   References

ACHEBE, C. (1972) 'What do African intellectuals read?', *The Times Literary Supplement*, 12 May.

ACHEBE, C. (1973) 'The role of the writer in a new nation' in KILLAM, G. (ed.) *African Writers on African Writings*, Heinemann.

ACHEBE, C. (1983) *The Trouble with Nigeria*, Heinemann.

ACHEBE, C. (1988) *Hopes and Impediments: selected essays, 1965–87*, Heinemann.

ASHCROFT, B., GRIFFITHS, G. and TIFFIN, H. (1989) *The Empire Writes Back: theory and practice in post-colonial literatures*, Routledge.

BAUGH, E. (ed.) (1978a) *Critics on Caribbean Literature*, Allen and Unwin.

BAUGH, E. (1978b) *Derek Walcott – Memory as Vision: Another life*, Longman.

BELSEY, C. (1980) *Critical Practice*, Methuen.

BRATHWAITE, E.K. (1984) *History of the Voice*, New Beacon.

BROWN, S. (1988/9) 'Spoiler, Walcott's People's Patriot', *Wasafiri*, 9.

CARY, J. (1965) *Mister Johnson*, Penguin.

CHINWEIZU, JEMIE, O. and MADUBUIKE, I. (1980/5) *Toward the Decolonization of African Literature*, KPI/Routledge.

CONRAD, J. (1971, 2nd edn) *Heart of Darkness*, Norton (first published 1899).

CUDJOE, S.R. (1988) *V.S. Naipaul: a materialist reading*, University of Massachusetts Press.

DABYDEEN, D. (1984) *Slave Song*, Dangaroo (Denmark).

DABYDEEN, D. (1989) 'On not being Milton: Nigger talk in England today', *Landfall*, 170, New Zealand.

DABYDEEN, D. and WILSON-TAGOE, N. (1988) *A Reader's Guide to West Indian and Black British Literature*, Hansib/Rutherford.

EAGLETON, T. (1983) *Literary Theory: an introduction*, Basil Blackwell.

FANON, F. (1967) (trans. Farrington, C.) *The Wretched of the Earth*, Penguin (first published in French, 1961).

FANON, F. (1986) (trans. Markmann, C.) *Black Skin, White Masks*, Pluto.

FORD, B. (ed.) (1983) *New Pelican Guide to English Literature: Vol.8, The Present*, Penguin.

FRANK, K. (1987) 'Women without men: the feminist novel in Africa' in JONES, E.D., PALMER, E. and JONES, L. (eds) *Women in African Literature Today*, Heinemann.

GILROY, B. (1989) 'The woman writer and commitment', *Wasafiri*, 10.

GORDIMER, N. (1971) 'White expatriates and black mimics: *In a Free State*', *New York Times Book Review*, 17 October.

GRAMSCI, A. (1986) (trans. Hoare, Q. and Nowell-Smith, G.) *Selections from the Prison Notebooks*, Lawrence and Wishart.

GRIFFITHS, G. (1978) *A Double Exile: African and West Indian writing between two cultures*, Marion Boyars.

HAMNER, R.D. (ed.) (1977) *Critical Perspectives on V.S. Naipaul*, Heinemann.

HEANEY, S. (1989) *The Government of the Tongue*, Faber.

JAMES, C.L.R. (1963) *The Black Jacobins*, Paladin.

LAMMING, G. (1960) *The Pleasures of Exile*, Paladin.

LINDFORS, B. (1975) 'National literatures in Africa', *English in Africa*, 2.

MAJA-PEARCE, A. (1985) 'The Naipauls on Africa: an African view', *Journal of Commonwealth Literature*, XX(1).

MILLER, J. (1990) *Seductions: studies in reading and culture*, Virago.

MOORE, G. (1978) *Wole Soyinka*, Evans.

NAIPAUL, V.S. (1965) 'Images', *New Statesman*, 24 September.

NAIPAUL, V.S. (1968) *An Area of Darkness*, Penguin.

NAIPAUL, V.S. (1969a) *The Suffrage of Elvira*, Penguin.

NAIPAUL, V.S. (1969b) *The Middle Passage*, Penguin (first published 1962).

NAIPAUL, V.S. (1971) *Miguel Street*, Penguin.

NAIPAUL, V.S. (1976) *The Overcrowded Barracoon*, Penguin.

NAIPAUL, V.S. (1979) *India: a wounded civilization*, Penguin.

NAIPAUL, V.S. (1987) *The Enigma of Arrival*, Penguin.

NAIPAUL, V.S. (1990) *India: a million mutinies now*, Heinemann.

NARAYAN, R.K. (1938) *The Dark Room*, Macmillan.

NARAYAN, R.K. (1945) *The English Teacher*, Eyre and Spottiswoode.

NARAYAN, R.K. (1988) *A Writer's Nightmare: selected essays, 1958–1988*, Penguin.

NARAYAN, R.K. (1989) *My Days: a memoir*, Penguin.

NGUGI, WA THIONG'O (1986) *Decolonizing the Mind*, Currey/Heinemann.

NICHOLS, G. (1983) *I is a Long-memoried Woman*, Karnak.

NICHOLS, G. (1984) *The Fat Black Woman's Poems*, Virago.

NICHOLS, G. (1988) 'In conversation with Maggie Butcher', *Wasafiri*, 8.

NICHOLS, G. (1989) *Lazy Thoughts of a Lazy Woman*, Virago.

NIGHTINGALE, P. (1987) *Journey Through Darkness: the writing of V.S. Naipaul*, University of Queensland Press.

OGUNDIPE-LESLIE, M. (1987) 'The female writer and her commitment' in JONES, E.D., PALMER, E. and JONES, L. (eds) *Women in African Literature Today*, Heinemann.

RAMCHAND, K. (1973, 2nd edn) *The West Indian Novel and its Background*, Heinemann.

RAO, V.P. (1971) 'Tea with R.K. Narayan', *Journal of Commonwealth Literature*, VI(1).

SINFIELD, A. (ed.) (1983) *Society and Literature 1945–1970*, Methuen.

SIVANANDAN, A. (1990) 'The enigma of the colonized: reflections on Naipaul's arrival', *Race and Class*, XXXII(1).

SOUTH BANK SHOW (1989) 'Derek Walcott', a film produced and directed by Tony Knox.

SOYINKA, W. (1981) *Aké: the years of childhood*, Arena/Collins.

SOYINKA, W. (1985) *The Man Died: prison notes*, Arrow/Hutchinson.

THIEME, J. (1987) *The Web of Tradition: uses of allusion in V.S. Naipaul's fiction*, Hansib/Dangaroo.

WALCOTT, D. (1972) 'What the twilight says: an overture', *Dream on Monkey Mountain and other Plays*, Cape.

WALCOTT, D. (1976) *Sea Grapes*, Cape.

WALCOTT, D. (1981) *The Fortunate Traveller*, Faber.

WALCOTT, D. (1986) *Collected Poems*, Faber.

WALCOTT, D. (1987) *The Arkansas Testament*, Faber.

WALCOTT, D. (1988) interview, *The Guardian*, 9 July.

WALCOTT, D. (1990) *Omeros*, Faber.

WALSH, W. (1990) *Indian Literature in English*, Longman.

WATERHOUSE, K. (1960) 'New novels', *New Statesman*, 17 September.

WHITE, L. (1975) *V.S. Naipaul: a critical introduction*, Macmillan.

WREN, R. (1980) *Achebe's World*, Longman.

Acknowledgements

Grateful acknowledgement is made to the following for permission to reproduce material in this block:

Walcott, D., excerpts from *Collected Poems* and 'Names' from *Sea Grapes*, copyright © 1974, 1976 by Derek Walcott, reprinted by permission of Faber and Faber Ltd (1986) and Farrar, Straus and Giroux Inc; Soyinka, W. (1985) *The Man Died: prison notes*, by permission of Rex Collings. The Yoruba songs from *Madmen and Specialists* were translated by Kole Omotoso, University of Ile-Ife.

BLOCK 6
NEW WRITINGS

Cover illustration: West African wall decoration, carved ebony, *c.*1940; private collection.